The HATCHER *Porcelain* CARGOES

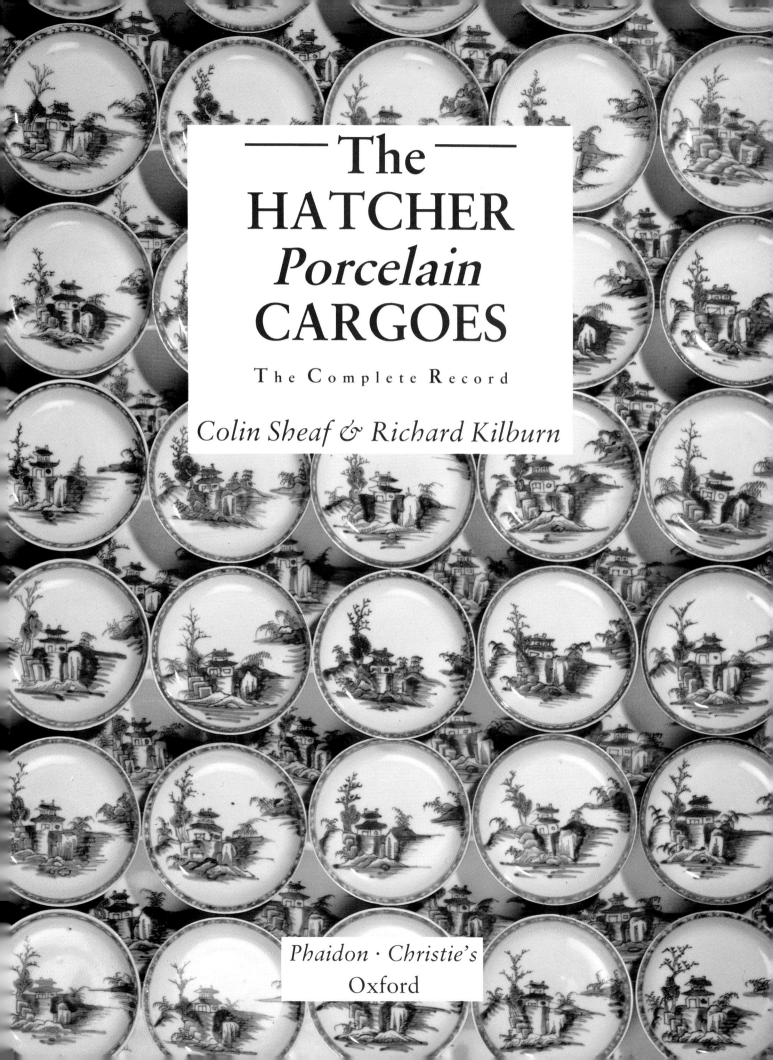

The HATCHER *Porcelain* CARGOES

The Complete Record

Colin Sheaf & Richard Kilburn

Phaidon · Christie's
Oxford

Phaidon · Christie's Limited
Littlegate House
St Ebbe's Street
Oxford
OX1 1SQ

First published 1988

British Library Cataloguing in Publication Data

The Hatcher porcelain cargoes: the complete
    record.
        1. Porcelain, Chinese — Ming-Ch'ing
    dynasties, 1368–1912 — Collectors
    and collecting
        I. Sheaf, Colin and Kilburn, Richard
    738.2'0951   NK4565.5

ISBN 0-7148-8046-9

Designed by Alan Moore

Printed in Holland by Onkenhout B.V. Hilversum

*Frontispiece. Blue and white Pagoda Riverscape pattern saucers,
from the cargo of the Geldermalsen, c.1750.*

ACKNOWLEDGEMENTS

The authors acknowledge the assistance given at all stages of the shipwreck recoveries by Captain
Michael Hatcher, Max de Rham, their associates, and the staff of United Subseas Services.

T. Volker and Dr Christian Jorg have provided, by their important researches into Dutch shipping and the VOC, rich sources of invaluable primary information on which this book repeatedly
draws.

While many collectors, dealers and art historians have contributed to the preparation of this book,
the authors are particularly grateful for assistance received from Sir Michael Butler, Michael and
Rosemary Cohen, Julia Curtis, David S. Howard and Christine van der Pijl-Ketel. Colleagues at
Christie's Amsterdam have been unfailingly helpful, notably Hetti Jongsma Blanche-Koelensmid,
Feng-chun Ma, Leila de Vos van Steenwijk and Dorrit Terwindt.

Without the enthusiasm and professional skills of Judy Walker, this project would have followed
the Asian junk and the *Geldermalsen* to a premature grave on an uncharted reef. Alan Moore successfully solved the complicated problems caused by the layout requirements, while Susannah Spicer
willingly processed disparate copy. The preparation of the Glossary owes much to the labours of
Margaret Medley.

**Unless otherwise credited in the captions, all photographs are reproduced by courtesy of
Christie's London and Christie's Amsterdam.**

CONTENTS

Pl. 1. A conger eel emerges from an
encrusted European stoneware jar on
the site of the *Geldermalsen*.

INTRODUCTION

No auctions of Chinese art at Christie's have had such an impact on academic studies and collectors as the dispersal of the ceramic contents of two shipwrecks, the Hatcher Junk (1643-6) and the *Geldermalsen* (1752). Recovered from the South China Seas, some 190,000 pieces of 'new' Chinese porcelain were successfully sold between 1983 and 1986 at auctions which gripped the attention of the art world and attracted many first-time buyers.

The subsequent dispersal throughout the world of the cargoes inevitably made study of the porcelain difficult. This book seeks to record an extensive group of these ceramics, ensuring that future collectors and scholars will have a context into which the porcelain may be set. The wide-ranging photographs illustrate the most noteworthy porcelain discoveries found on the two ships, an invaluable source of reference for collectors. Above all, *The Hatcher Porcelain Cargoes* aims to interpret these ceramics, which form by far the largest bulk of the objects recovered, to consider their significance within the evolution of Chinese porcelain forms and decorations, and to explain their presence within the historical context of Chinese porcelain production and the Asian shipping trade.

The news of Captain Michael Hatcher's sensational discoveries spread beyond the art world to the media and the general public. In future such salvage operations will become increasingly common as new deep-sea technology makes available, at ever greater depths, wrecks hitherto inaccessible to divers with conventional equipment. To find such wrecks requires considerable archival research, professional skill in surveying the seabed, and a substantial element of luck; a chance sonar observation can save weeks of tedious surveying, and a great deal of money.

The auctions capitalized on the excitement and romance of these lost cargoes, brought to life in the case of the *Geldermalsen* by the absorbing archive material assembled by Dr Christian Jorg, Keeper of the Groeningen Museum in northern Holland. Without the research undertaken and published by him, both on the *Geldermalsen* and more generally on the history of the Dutch East India Company's involvement with the Far East, neither of Captain Hatcher's ships would have benefited from the engrossing circumstantial historical detail which makes their contents particularly fascinating to collectors and academics. The contribution that his labours among the primary source materials have made to this book is gratefully acknowledged.

The auctions themselves were important for the art world. Christie's had to develop new methods to disperse these huge cargoes into – or preferably outside –

the collector market for Chinese porcelain, which was perceived to be fairly stable but very finite. Only by drawing the attention of the wider general public to the unique historical and documentary significance of each cargo, and illustrating the fascinating tale of their recovery, could the risk be avoided of flooding the established market with a colossal volume of somewhat indigestible material. Learning from his experience with the much less-documented first cargo, Captain Hatcher made greater efforts to record the course of the second salvage operation. By commissioning a video and stills photographer to record the entire *Geldermalsen* excavation, he provided valuable information both about the wreck site and the way the porcelain was stored; this at the same time gave Christie's the opportunity to prepare a promotional video which made many more potential purchasers aware of the fascinating background to the 'Nanking Cargo' than conventional art world advertising could have done.

There is a serious threat to thousands of untouched seabed historical sites if recovered artefacts can be sold for high prices without any effort being made to establish a context or to record the information properly. Ceramic historians and archaeologists will be grateful that, if the contents of the *Geldermalsen* were to be salvaged by a commercial salvor, it should have been one who took the trouble to draw scale plans of the site, to photograph as much as the murky, tea-filled water would permit, and who offered the opportunity (sadly not taken up) for a trained archaeologist to accompany the expedition. Shards were willingly recovered in some quantity, many eroded and of minimal commercial significance; a large group, as well as a study group of intact pieces, was presented by Hatcher's company to the Groeningen Museum. A further selection of shards was presented by Christie's Amsterdam. It would not have been possible to write this book if Captain Hatcher had not tried to record site details and preserve fragmentary artefacts. With his help, it is possible for this book to illustrate not a definitive but certainly a wide-ranging variety of the porcelain forms and decorations from both

Pl. 2. Potential purchasers wait patiently for the doors to open on the first day to view the 'Nanking Cargo'.

Pl. 3. A few encrusted plates and dishes from a unique blue and white octagonal service are all that survived the wreck of the *Geldermalsen*. S. Daw, *Plum Blossoms, Hong Kong*.

wrecks, instead of just the perfect, 'commercial' artefacts.

A photographic record of the porcelain, however wide-ranging, would be rather meaningless without some analysis. The major aim of this book is therefore to discuss the ceramics in greater detail than has been done hitherto, and to explain as far as possible how they were produced, marketed and used.

The earlier of the two vessels, known simply as the 'Asian junk' or the 'Hatcher junk', bore a fascinating cargo, dating from a moment of some obscurity in Chinese ceramic history. How fascinating it actually was, was not immediately appreciated by collectors in December 1983, when a 'trial selection' was offered in an auction at Christie's Amsterdam. The wares were obviously unusual, but the glaze of most of the pieces had been made dull and matt by sea salt and there was no historical background or provenance for this peculiar group of lots in the sale. Prices were low; the disappointing results suggested that future sales required fuller explanation of the origin and significance of this type of export porcelain if bidders were to be attracted. By the time of the second sale, in March 1984, the point had got across. Some of the world's most astute ceramic specialists – most notably, London's British Museum – began to assemble representative groups of the finest examples. The third sale, in June 1984, again achieved high prices, especially for the many ceramics which increased knowledge of the chronological development of seventeenth-century Chinese porcelain. This sale was presumed to be the last; the only other substantial unauctioned group was Michael Hatcher's personal collection, with many fine pieces culled from the recovered cargo of 25,000 objects. Initially kept for pleasure, fears for its safety led him to offer what was probably the last available small, but select, group. By February 1985, a new collector market had grown for this 'Hatcher shipwreck' porcelain; prices were higher than ever for porcelain now widely recognized as being from a sealed 'time capsule'. Pulling together illustrations of the more interesting pieces from each of

the four sales, this book sets out to place the 'Asian junk' wares firmly in the context of seventeenth-century ceramics.

Pl. 4. Captain Michael Hatcher (left) surrounded by tiers of *Geldermalsen* porcelain safely delivered to Amsterdam after two centuries.

Few major dealers had bought these less-appreciated early wares, meaning that a number of new buyers had been able to make what turned out to be excellent purchases. The announcement at a Press conference in January 1986 of the discovery and forthcoming auction of a second shipwreck of porcelain, provisionally named the 'Nanking Cargo', led many collectors to hope that there would be equally good buys. The sale represented the commercial cargo of an unidentified European merchant ship, returning from China in the mid-eighteenth century. All 150,000 pieces of porcelain were to be offered in one five-day auction, together with gold bars and other artefacts. There were prospects for splendid bargains, because the huge volume of porcelain had led Christie's to predict extremely reasonable sale prices.

But there were few bargains for the thousands of hopeful bidders when the sale began on 28 April 1986; no bargains that day, or indeed any other. Early risers joined the long queues already forming at 8.00 am at the 'paddle registration' desk outside the salerooms in the Amsterdam Hilton. In the main saleroom itself, television crews from twelve networks jostled for the best vantage points on the Press plinth raised to the right of the auctioneer's rostrum. The main room and a subsidiary saleroom at the far end, hung appropriately with great diagonal swathes of blue and white cloth, were banked along the sides with closed-circuit television monitors, to illustrate each type of lot being offered so that bidders with an incomplete view of the rostrum could be certain they were buying the right thing. All 600 seats had long been reserved, but several hundred more bidders

stood along the walls by the time that John Gloyne, one of an international Christie's team of seven auctioneers, rapped his gavel for silence before the first of the 2,849 lots on offer.

For Michael Hatcher and his colleagues, it was the successful culmination of a long salvage project which had threatened to founder on a number of occasions. For Christie's, and especially for the staff of Christie's Amsterdam saleroom, it was the culmination of a professional exercise on a scale unmatched in two hundred years of auctioneering: nine months of organizing, cataloguing and marketing probably the largest group of ceramics offered at an international auction since the heyday of the eighteenth-century European trade with China.

The results of the sale are now history. For Captain Hatcher and United Subsea Services, their huge personal investments of time and capital saw dividends four and five times greater than the printed auction estimates led them reasonably to expect; the sale was to total slightly over an astonishing £10 million. Some 5,000 bidders registered to take part in person at the auction, and over 12,000 catalogues were circulated in advance. The massive pre-sale Press coverage generated such intense international interest from people who had barely heard of Chinese export porcelain before, much less collected it, that well over 100,000 'absentee commission' written bids were received from around the world. Christie's Paris office held the individual record for bids received locally on any single day; the telex containing commission bids, two days before the sale, was nearly twenty feet long.

There could hardly have been a more satisfactory result from the 'Nanking Cargo' dispersal; every single lot in the sale was sold, normally at several times the high estimate. The 'Cargo' had become the most successful single auction ever held of a collection of decorative arts.

The Press coverage, though enormous, was somewhat simplistic, stressing the romance of the cargo without being much concerned with the objects in detail. Among the tens of thousands of new owners of tea and dinner service porcelain, relatively few are aware of the fascinating historical circumstances which gave rise to huge, uneventful annual shipments from Canton of 'China trade' goods, including *Geldermalsen*-type porcelain. To provide that context, this book explains the history of Chinese export porcelain. Greater understanding of the nature and origin of these fine-quality, if unexceptional, ceramics can only give us a fuller appreciation of our extraordinary good luck, that the *Geldermalsen* should have survived such a fatal accident with so many of her contents intact.

THE HATCHER JUNK *(1643–6)*

SEABORNE TRADE BETWEEN CHINA AND SOUTH-EAST ASIA

In order to place the porcelain recovered from the Hatcher junk into its seventeenth-century historical and ceramic context, we shall first look briefly at the seaborne trade between China and South-East Asia and at what little we know or can infer about the organization of the potteries at Jingdezhen at the end of the Ming dynasty.

As early as the eighth century, Persian and Arab merchants had developed trade links between the Middle East, India, South-East Asian ports and China.[1] There were large colonies of these merchants in Canton and other port cities. They paid taxes to the government and no doubt ensured their welcome by giving large presents to local officials, but it was not until the Southern Song dynasty that trade dues became an important part of government revenue.

From the eleventh and twelfth centuries, Chinese from the southern coastal provinces of Fujian and Guangdong became increasingly involved in private seaborne trade, sailing their junks on regular trading voyages throughout the South-East Asian archipelago and establishing Chinese communities in numerous small ports. This trade gave rise to the manufacture of the brown, white and celadon wares, as well as blue and white after about 1300, made specifically for export and excavated today in such quantities in the Philippines, Indonesia, Malaysia and Thailand.

The seven great expeditions undertaken by the eunuch Zheng He in the early fifteenth century represent the high point of China's influence as a maritime power.[2] The first grand fleet departed in 1405, with 28,000 men carried in sixty-two vessels, and sailed as far as India. Subsequent expeditions reached Hormuz on the Persian Gulf, Aden at the entrance to the Red Sea, and various Arab ports down the east African coast as far south as Zanzibar. The object of these expeditions was primarily to overawe the local rulers of the states they visited, and to induce them to acknowledge allegiance to the Emperor by sending regular tribute missions to Beijing. Several rulers did indeed visit China personally and were

Pl. 6. A group of pieces from the Hatcher junk in Christie's warehouse in Amsterdam, ready for auction.

magnificently received, including two from Palembang and Ceylon who were brought back forcibly to witness the splendour of the Son of Heaven. However, the ambassadors were increasingly often Court officials, sometimes of Chinese origin themselves, whose real purpose was to trade.

The tribute system became expanded over the years into a highly flexible arrangement, within which trade on a large scale could be conducted. By the end of the seventeenth century, the King of Thailand had by gradual stages negotiated permission for an Embassy to arrive at Canton with three or more vessels.[3] While the official party were in Beijing, which was likely to be for six to eight months, the ships would return to Ayuthia. A further return journey might be caused by the need for repairs or some other emergency, and on each trip permission would be given for a 'ballast' cargo to be loaded, supposedly to ensure the vessel's stability. By these contrived means, twelve or more shiploads of cargo could be carried in each direction. The number of vessels and return voyages, how much of the cargo could be considered as tribute goods, how much was 'ballast', and the prices and levels of duty were the subject of much delicate negotiation. The arrangement suited both parties since it kept the trade under official control, brought in revenue from duties, and created a monopoly on various types of goods which each ruler could dispense to his further advantage, as European monarchs of the time were also accustomed to doing.

Such subtleties were beyond the patience of the European nations when they arrived in Asia. The tribute system did in fact represent a formula for government-controlled rather than private trade, which would certainly have suited the European governments and East India Companies admirably if they had understood its potential, but no European ruler could have brought himself to acknowledge even a nominal subservience to the Emperor and particularly not in the humiliating terms required by the rigid Court protocol governing tribute embassies.

In any case, from the first arrival of the Portuguese on the China coast early in the sixteenth century, it was clear that not only had the great Ming navy of a hundred years before ceased to exist, but the Chinese were no longer able to protect their own shores. The Portuguese took advantage of this situation by persistently sending vessels to carry on illicit trade with local merchants at pre-arranged meeting points along the coast, until the provincial authorities were forced to allow them to settle at Macao in 1557 in order to bring their activities under official supervision.

The reasons for the decline of China as a maritime power are too complex to discuss in detail in this brief survey. They involved the need to concentrate all resources and attention on the northern borders, again under threat from the Mongols, and to close off the southern coasts from undesirable foreign influences, except for official tribute embassies, which could be closely monitored. A deeper cause was the entrenched opposition to any form of commerce among the official classes, whose power derived from the ownership of land and their control of administrative and tax-gathering functions. They were able to argue against commercialism on good Confucian grounds, pointing out that tribute and private trade only brought unnecessary luxuries into the country and that Zheng He's expeditions were vastly expensive. Moreover, most of the profits from private trade did not reach the official coffers but simply enriched the despised merchant class whose newfound wealth tended to disturb the old order of society. It was an attitude that would have been readily understood by members of the Whig landed gentry in eighteenth-century England. The once-powerful Ming navy was starved of funds and simply allowed to waste away. Joseph Needham tells us that 'by 1474, only 140 warships of the main fleet of 400 were left. By 1503, the Tengchow

Pl. 7. 'Batavia: Governour's House within the Castle' from Jan Nieuhoff, *An Embassy from the East India, Company of the United Provinces to the Grand Tarter Cham, Emperor of China,* 1st English edition, 1669. 34 × 27.5 cm.

squadron had dropped from 100 vessels to 10. Desertion occurred wholesale and the corps of shipwrights disintegrated.'[4]

The suppression of private trade was already taking place before the first of Zheng He's expeditions set out.[5] A series of progressively more severe edicts forbade the building of ocean-going vessels, and prohibited the Chinese from going abroad or entering into foreign trade on pain of death. The last grand fleet returned in 1433 and private trade must have been severely curtailed by that date, although it is difficult to judge how completely effective the ban was.

The coastal population had come to depend on overseas trade and shipbuilding for their livelihood, so that the effect of the ban must have been disastrous. The coastal regions of Fujian and Guangdong, apart from the Pearl river estuary, are mountainous and barren, with insufficient cultivable land to support a large population. Many Chinese would have had relatives living abroad in the ports to which their junks sailed each year, who would have been cut off by the termination of the annual voyages. Thus, as the ability of the central government to control the coastal provinces weakened, private shipbuilding resumed, clandestine voyages were again made and smuggling networks developed inland to collect and distribute trade goods. By the Chenghua period (1465–87), there are references to members of the local gentry owning vessels, and a Korean official passing Hangzhou in 1487 reported that 'foreign [presumably foreign-going] ships stand as thick as the teeth of a comb'.[6]

A measure of the decline and revival of the junk trade can be seen in the shards of export ware found throughout South-East Asia. There is a clear gap between the fourteenth-century types and the appearance of a quite different group of blue and white ware which has not yet been dated accurately, although the shapes and decorative motifs can be related to pieces with Hongzhi (1488–1505) and Zhengde (1506–21) reign marks.

The Portuguese Duarte Barbosa, whose famous book of his travels was completed in about 1518, visited a trading port named Reynel situated on the Tapti river north of the modern Bombay. He recorded that 'the Moors who dwell here are wealthy and distinguished, fair in colour and of gentle birth. They go well attired, their women are beautiful and they have good houses, well kept and furnished. They use, in the front room of their houses, to have many shelves all round, the whole room being surrounded by them as in a shop, all filled with fair and rich porcelain of new styles.'[7] At this time, such porcelain would have come through one of the transhipment ports such as Malacca or Ayuthia, where Moslem and Chinese merchants met to exchange their wares.

There were five Chinese junks in port when the Portuguese first arrived at Malacca in 1509.[8] Several writers, such as Tome Pires, noted their activities in a wide range of South-East Asian ports in their reports on the commercial possibilities of the region during the second decade of the fifteenth century.[9] However, once they were able to obtain Chinese goods through Macao, their initially friendly relations with the Chinese junk masters changed to a policy of trying to force all vessels passing through the Straits to put into Malacca, where extortionate duties were extracted.[10] The arrival of the aggressive Europeans broke the Chinese dominance of trade in the region and created uncertain and sometimes dangerous trading conditions, but the overall effect was a massive expansion of the market, of which the Chinese were always the best organized to take advantage.

In 1567, the Chinese government's attitude to private trade finally changed. Fifty licences were issued for overseas voyages in that year, increasing to 100 in 1575 and to 137 early in the seventeenth century. We may take it that the licences were issued in an attempt to regulate a *de facto* situation beyond the authorities' control, and that additional voyages continued to be made. The official figures nevertheless give us some idea of the pattern of the trade. Among the vessels licensed in 1589, sixteen went to Manila, eleven to Vietnam, five to Thailand, four each to Bantam and Palembang, and one or two each to a wide range of other ports.[11]

The Dutch arrived in the area in 1596 and quickly displaced the Portuguese as the dominant sea power. A regional headquarters was established at Batavia in 1621 and the Chinese were actively encouraged to come there rather than to Bantam, which was then the busiest entrepot port in the region, particularly for pepper and other Indonesian products.[12] The Dutch failed to gain permission to trade with China, and an attempt to capture Macao in 1622 was fought off by the Portuguese. However, they were able to build a fortified trading post on the off-shore island of Taiwan in 1624, from where they could order most of the Chinese products they required, including fine porcelain for the European, Indian and Middle Eastern markets.

Despite this, a large and influential Chinese community quickly settled in Batavia. The Dutch authorities recognized that much of the port's success depended upon the Chinese ability to carry on inter-island trade through their own established networks, at prices with which the Dutch themselves could not compete. After initially trying to gain a complete monopoly by strong-arm tactics, the Dutch were content by the 1640s to encourage regional trade through Batavia; to sell protection, in the form of trading licences, to junks passing through areas

Pl. 8. Dutch still life. Circle of Bahrend van der Meer (born c.1659).

patrolled by their vessels; and to attempt to retain monopolies on return cargoes to Europe wherever possible, only entering into regional trade in commodities they could control. Even to Europe, a complete monopoly could never be maintained. The English were able to buy pepper, spices and porcelain in Bantam, and the Spanish were the largest buyers of fine Chinese silks, which they shipped home via the Americas.[13]

Chinese goods brought to the market at Batavia each year included copper and iron utensils, such as cooking pots, nails and needles, raw and woven silk of various qualities, and other fabrics, including damask, satin, brocade and coarse textiles. There were also handicrafts, such as lacquer boxes and cabinets, fans, paper, and fine and coarse porcelain in large quantities. Bulk items were salt, unrefined sugar, saltpetre, sulphur and temperate-climate fruits. The Chinese came to buy pepper, for which the demand was enormous. They also bought other spices, medicinal herbs, sandalwood, camphor and other fancy woods, resin, semi-precious stones, ivory and horn, Indian cotton cloth and European woollens.

The Chinese junks making the voyage to Batavia or Bantam varied in size between 200 and 800 tonnes. The voyage from the China coast took about three weeks and would normally be made in December or January, while the favourable north-east monsoon was blowing, returning in June or July when the wind was from the south-west. Thus only one voyage could be made in each trading season, since the junks were not well designed for tacking against the wind.[14]

The deck and 'tween deck was divided into many small cabins and storage areas in which merchants and small pedlars could travel with their goods. The captain and crew were usually not paid, but took part in the profitability of the voyage or were allocated space for their own cargoes. Two or three hundred poor Chinese emigrants travelled as deck passengers on each voyage, usually being contracted to work for whoever paid their passage.

It was possible to invest a sum of money with a merchant planning to purchase, let us say, a consignment of porcelain, the proceeds from which would be used to buy pepper for the return voyage. The prices for each commodity fluctuated considerably, but the investor might expect a profit of 50 to 100 per cent on his outlay if all went well. In days when there were no banks or insurance companies, it was a means of raising finance for a commercial venture and of spreading the risk. It was a more direct, and a riskier, form of investment than the European joint stock companies of the time, such as the East India Companies (see page 82), which functioned on an institutional basis, the stockholder being paid a dividend on the annual results rather than on the profit or loss from a particular transaction.

The junk trade had been developed by members of the landed gentry in the coastal areas, who would make use of the manpower and resources of their clan or lineage association to build and operate ocean-going vessels.[15] Members of the clan or their trusted servants would purchase suitable trade goods and travel with the vessel, while others would take up residence in the overseas ports with which they traded in order to manage the business arrangements at that end. As they prospered and were able to operate more junks, co-operation with other groups became necessary in order to expand, finance and protect the particular trade in which they were involved. Influence with the provincial authorities would also have been essential in order to be able to ship their goods, legally or illegally, with the minimum payment of dues or official interference.

Thus large trading organizations grew up, of which the greatest was the Cheng family, who by the 1640s seem to have established a degree of control over the entire junk trade. This was no doubt a loose control based on the co-operation of many independent junk owners and merchants, and involving the combined efforts of large numbers of the coastal population. Their organization was to form the strongest and longest-lasting political force to support the Ming after they had been driven from Beijing by the Manzus. From 1645 to 1680, it dominated the coasts of Fujian and Guangdong provinces, raising fleets and armies which defied the efforts of the Manzus to bring these areas under their government.

THE PORCELAIN INDUSTRY AT JINGDEZHEN DURING THE MING DYNASTY

The district of Fouliang in north-eastern Jiangxi province, in which Jingdezhen is situated, is known to have supplied porcellanous stoneware to the Palace as early as the sixth century. However, it did not become one of the better-known pottery regions until the eleventh and twelfth centuries, when the local deposits of China clay (kaolin) and China stone (petuntse) were refined to produce a white porcelain known as Yingqing ware.

At some time around 1300, underglaze blue decoration was introduced and it was this innovation which was to elevate Jingdezhen into China's leading ceramic centre. The early blue and white wares seem to have been made mainly for export to the Middle East: large, handsome dishes, bowls and vases decorated with Chinese motifs, but arranged into banded and segmented patterns derived from Islamic wares. Blue decorations were also added to smaller, humbler white wares, on shapes for which there was a well-established demand in the South-East Asian ports served by the junk trade. The famous David temple vases,[16] with inscriptions dated 1351, show that the wares were appreciated in China itself, but they were initially considered in Court circles to be less refined than the finest white wares and did not come into Imperial favour until the Yongle period (1403–24), when a new decorative style was designed which was more in keeping with Chinese tastes.

Porcelain-making was a seasonal industry, for a number of reasons connected

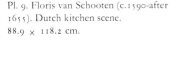

Pl. 9. Floris van Schooten (c.1590-after 1655). Dutch kitchen scene. 88.9 × 118.2 cm.

both with the manufacturing process and with transportation. The clay was mined in the spring and early summer, and broken into lumps before being sold to the crushers. A treatise on porcelain of 1815 tells us that 'above Wang Chiang on the east of the Town (of Jingdezhen) there are twenty-eight rapids, each one of which has a water-driven pestle . . . In the spring when there is a lot of water each shed can operate all its pestles, but later in the year when there is less water and the power is reduced, several pestles are cut out. When the force of the water is even, the pounded earth is dense and fine, but when the water runs slowly and the power is light, the pounded earth tends to be coarse.'[17] The clay was then moulded into bricks, dried and delivered to the potteries by wheelbarrow. There the kaolin and petuntse were mixed according to the quality of the porcelain required, pounded for a day, placed in large water jars for a settling process, dried, sieved, pounded again to remove the air bubbles and remoulded into bricks of suitable size for the potters to handle.[18] The actual throwing and glazing of the pots had to take place during the summer and autumn months because the clay would became rock hard and the glaze would turn opaque in China's winter temperatures.

Porcelain for overseas markets was transported to the coast mainly by water, involving several transhipments from one craft to another, which must have made the costs and the risk of breakages high. The cargo was first loaded into a river craft to be shipped down to Poyang Lake, then into a larger craft to cross the lake and back into a smaller one for the journey down the Gan river. It was then carried over the Meiling Pass on poles, a portage of eight or nine hours, before being reshipped to Canton or Fujian ports. During the winter months, shipments could be delayed by a drop in the level of water at shallow points along the route.[19] As we saw above, the junk trade was itself seasonal, to fit in with the monsoons and to avoid typhoons, which normally strike the south China coast in spring and early summer.

At the end of the Ming dynasty, the potteries were still mainly small family workshops, many of which did not even have their own kilns.[20] This had arisen, at

Pl. 10. The stages of porcelain manufacture. Anglo-Chinese School, c.1800. 103.2 × 189.9 cm. Note the waterwheel (left) driving the pestles to pulverize the clay.

least partially, from the way in which the Imperial orders were placed. There was no Imperial factory, in the sense of a pottery owned by the Emperor or managed by his retainers. An Imperial depot was first established in 1425 under the supervision of a eunuch commissioner, whose function was to place the annual orders with privately owned pottery workshops designated as 'official'.[21] The number of these 'official' workshops was increased from twenty to fifty-eight during the Xuande period (1426–35).[22] The need for such a large number of kilns is explained by the record of an order in 1433 for 443,500 pieces.[23] These wares were, of course, not all intended for the Palace. They would have been distributed throughout the administrative hierarchy and used as gifts by the Emperor and his officials, both internally in China and to visiting tribute embassies.

Imperial interest in and demand for porcelain was substantially less during the middle decades of the fifteenth century, reviving in the Chenghua period (1465–89). The gradual re-emergence of the junk trade from this time also brought a new demand for export wares, and the volume of orders built up progressively during the sixteenth century. The growth in Imperial orders can be seen from the following figures:[24]

	Number of pieces fired
1529	2,570
1531	12,300
1544	50,000
1555	79,750
1571	105,770
1577	174,700

At the same time, the practice grew up of contracting out 'Imperial gift' wares to non-official private kilns, leaving the 'official' potteries to produce the finest wares for use in the Palace. By the Wanli period (1573–1619), the number of 'official' potteries had been reduced to twenty.[25]

The arrival of the Portuguese in Asia, followed by the Spanish, Dutch and English,[26] created an enormous new demand for export wares, with the difference that the Europeans wanted fine porcelain and were not satisfied with the coarser export types. We have no records to indicate the quantities being exported during the sixteenth century, but a Portuguese carrack captured by the Dutch in 1603 had an estimated 100,000 pieces on board,[27] which were auctioned in Amsterdam and created an even greater sensation than the Hatcher cargoes were to do 380 years later. The earliest of the Dutch annual orders for which we have a record was for 108,200 pieces in 1608 and this had grown to 355,800 pieces – for the European market alone – in 1644.[28]

The Imperial wares had been produced largely by requisitioning materials and completed pots in payment of tax obligations, with the potters and other workers being required to give *corvée* labour service, which during the early sixteenth century usually amounted to three months every fourth year.[29] However, a money economy was gradually appearing in China, and the Single Whip reforms of the 1560s led to tax and labour obligations being settled in cash. The Imperial orders therefore also began to be paid for in cash.[30]

Porcelain-making was thus a seasonal and highly labour-intensive industry. During the summer months, a large pool of skilled and unskilled labour was required by potteries with orders to fulfil, drawing in to Jingdezhen men from the surrounding districts eager to earn a daily wage.[31] The industry became focussed in Jingdezhen itself as the source of orders and of labour to carry them out, in addition to its original role as the central market and clearing house for finished porcelain. This change led to the closure of many of the potteries which had grown up in outlying areas near to the sources of the China clay. Kilns such as Hutian[32] and Leping, which had been producing export wares for South-East Asian markets since southern Song times, ceased production during the second half of the sixteenth century as their skilled workers were attracted to Jingdezhen to help meet the demand for the more lucrative fine porcelain.

A Dutch report from Bantam dated 10 October 1616 states, 'You are herewith informed that the porcelains are made far inland in China, and the assortments which are sold to us and in these Native Quarters are put out to contract and made afterwards with money paid in advance, for in China assortments like these are not in use.'[33] It was usual practice for a merchant wishing to order a batch of porcelain to advance the money needed to buy semi-processed kaolin and petuntse, cobalt and wood for the firing. He would thus implicitly accept the considerable risk of losses caused by firing mishaps. In one of his letters from Jingdezhen in 1712 and 1722, Père D'Entrecolles wrote that 'it is rare for a furnace to succeed completely; often everything is lost, and on opening it the porcelain and the cases will be found converted into a solid mass as hard as a rock.'[34]

The potteries themselves were generally not able to finance their own production. They had developed as processors of specific Imperial and export orders rather than as independent businesses such as the Delft or Worcester factories in Europe, which had to design, finance, manufacture, distribute and sell their wares in order to return a profit on their initial outlay in equipment and materials. The owner of a small Jingdezhen pottery contributed only the labour of his family, servants and apprentices, the use of his equipment and the cost of any labour he hired for the contract.

This is, of course, an over-simplified picture. The financial arrangements must have been many and various. There must have been successful potteries operating on a larger scale with a certain amount of working capital. For example, we know that as early as 1608 the Dutch had been able to place an order which included 'porcelains, 50,000 butter-dishes, fine, 50,000 *telyooren* (plates), fine'.[35] These would have been Kraak wares, which had been in production since the 1570s or before, although probably not in such quantities. However, an order for 50,000 pieces of a single item implies the ability to mass-produce on a large scale and suggests that a private factory of substantial size was already in existence.

An interesting question is when fine porcelain was first designed specifically for the domestic market in China, other than to meet Imperial orders. It would seem that the potteries were permitted to sell off the remainder of the 'Imperial gift' wares, provided they did not bear the Emperor's reign mark, after the finest pieces had been selected for shipment to Beijing. They could also presumably make additional pieces in the same styles for commercial sale. No doubt the Imperial wares carried a prestige within China which made it unnecessary to introduce new and untried designs, but it may also be that the development of a domestic market lacked any commercial organization able to perceive that a demand existed and to finance and distribute a new 'line' of porcelain. Certainly, it is difficult to identify sixteenth-century types designed specifically for the domestic market rather than as Imperial or export wares.

The role of the merchants was crucial to the development of Jingdezhen, particularly after Imperial orders came to a halt following the death of the Emperor Wanli in 1620. They had long been active as middlemen for the Europeans, who were of course unable to enter China. They carried the orders to

Pl. 11. China and South-East Asia, showing Jingdezhen, the route to the coast and the main ports involved in the junk trade.

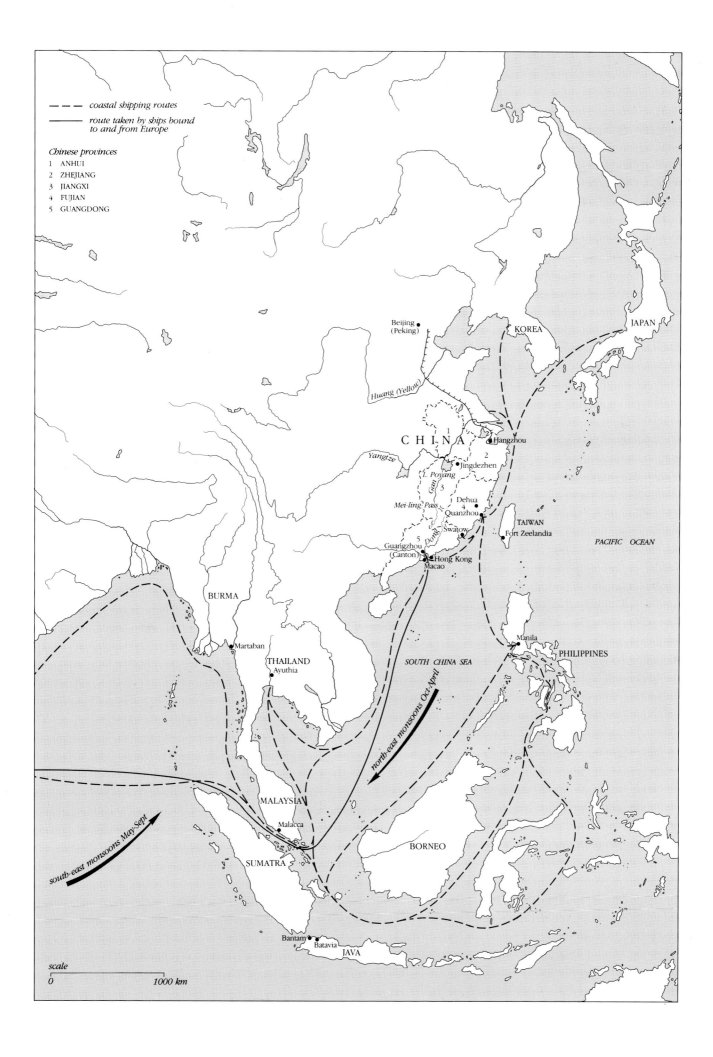

- - - - - *coastal shipping routes*
——— *route taken by ships bound
to and from Europe*

Chinese provinces
1 ANHUI
2 ZHEJIANG
3 JIANGXI
4 FUJIAN
5 GUANGDONG

Beijing
(Peking)

KOREA

JAPAN

Huang (Yellow)

C H I N A
1
Yangtze
2 Hangzhou
L. Poyang
Gan Jingdezhen
3
Mei-ling Pass Dehua
4 Quanzhou
Dong Swatow
5
Guangzhou
(Canton) Hong Kong
Macao

TAIWAN
Fort Zeelandia

PACIFIC OCEAN

BURMA

Martaban

THAILAND
Ayuthia

SOUTH CHINA SEA

Manila

PHILIPPINES

north-east monsoons Oct.-April

MALAYSIA

Malacca

south-east monsoons May-Sept.

SUMATRA

BORNEO

Bantam
Batavia
JAVA

scale
0   1000 km

Jingdezhen, financed the manufacture, organized transportation and accepted the risk of kiln losses, damage in transit or problems in obtaining payment. The Dutch seem to have agreed prices when placing their orders, but these were subject to the quality of the goods delivered. A consignment of porcelain brought to the wholesale markets of Batavia or Bantam would be sold at a constantly fluctuating price, depending on the season, the number of ships in port or expected, and the amount of porcelain in the market at the time. There might be a sudden surplus of brandy cups in Holland, or an urgent demand for tea cups of a certain shape in India, which the merchant would only find out when he arrived from China with that season's stock, with no prospect of adjusting to it until the following year.

Once the Imperial orders ceased, porcelain suitable for the domestic market would only have been made if this kind of entrepreneurial activity was undertaken. It seems that the potteries were unlikely to have been capable of it themselves, for the historical reasons we have discussed. Established styles could go on being produced, but the quality of Imperial wares had been in decline for several decades. An excellent commercial opportunity therefore arose to utilize the highly developed skills of the 'official' workshops. It would seem that, in order to take advantage of this, a carefully designed range of wares in new shapes and with lively new pictorial decorations was introduced, clearly intended for the domestic market. These are the Transitional wares, whose development is discussed below. They are especially interesting to us in this context because there were large numbers of them on board the Hatcher junk.

So who might have been responsible for introducing these wares? A likely candidate, or group of candidates, would be the Huizhou merchants. They came from a district of that name in the southern part of Anhui province, about a hundred miles north-east of Jingdezhen. They had been well-known as traders since Southern Song times, but by the seventeenth century they and a few other similar groups had become enormously wealthy and powerful. The foundation of their business was the salt monopoly, for which they were one of the main licensees, purchasing salt from the government in exchange for silver, and distributing it throughout China. They also dealt in essential commodities such as rice, timber and foodstuffs on a large scale, supplying the needs of provinces not self-sufficient in these products.[36]

China had been evolving slowly towards a money-based economy, but the process was accelerated dramatically by the arrival of the Europeans on the Asian trading scene. The English adventurer Ralph Fitch, who visited the East in 1585–91, wrote that 'when the Portugales goe from Macao in China to Japan, they carrie much white silke, Gold, Muske and Porcelanes; and they bring from thence nothing but Silver. They have a great Carake which goeth thither every yeare, and she bringeth from thence every yeare above 600,000 crusadoes, and all this silver of Japan, and 200,000 crusadoes more in Silver which they bring yearly out of India, they imploy to their great advantage in China.'[37] The flow was increased still further by trade with the Spanish after they established themselves at Manila in 1571. The Manila galleon arrived each year with silver from the mines in Mexico and Peru, which was used to buy silk, satin, brocades and other Chinese products. The import of silver from Manila in around 1600 has been estimated from Chinese customs revenues to have been a million taels per year or more.[38]

Huge quantities of silver thus came into China, most of which was in the hands of merchants rather than of the government. It is a commonplace of economic history that a large amount of money coming into circulation, particularly in a feudal society unable to absorb it into its existing economy, will give rise to a demand for, and therefore the manufacture of, luxury goods. A wide range of luxury goods were, of course, already being made in China, but the expansion of domestic demand gave a great stimulus to this process. The Huizhou merchants were at the centre of these activities. They had long been involved in the distribution of such items as paper, ink cakes, lacquerware, tea, silk and other fabrics. They also dealt in porcelain, books, woodblock prints and even Old Master paintings and other antiques.[39]

As their wealth grew during the later sixteenth and seventeenth centuries, the merchants are known to have financed the production and processing of luxury goods. To give two very different examples, factories were set up in Anhui for the starching and dyeing of cotton goods on a large scale, and the production of books and woodblock prints was financed and encouraged. It was from book illustrations and prints of the Anhui School that many of the new decorations on Transitional porcelain were drawn, although this does not prove any connection with the Huizhou merchants.

It would certainly be consistent with what we know of the Huizhou merchants' activities for them to seize the opportunity to make use of the 'official' porcelain kilns and even to commission designs for a new range of porcelain to be produced. Perhaps new historical evidence will emerge to throw further light on their activities and on the development of private factories at Jingdezhen.[40]

DATING THE SHIPWRECK AND THE PORCELAIN CARGO

Captain Hatcher's discovery of a wreck on a reef in the South China Sea containing a large shipment of seventeenth-century Chinese porcelain came at a time when there was widespread interest in the porcelain of the period. Since 1980, there have been no less than ten exhibitions in Britain, Holland, France, Belgium, the United States, Japan and Hong Kong, all with illustrated catalogues which discuss various aspects of seventeenth-century Chinese porcelain and make available photographs and descriptions of several hundred pieces from museums and private collections all over the world.[41]

Two other wrecks have recently been discovered, both of which had substantial quantities of porcelain on board, mostly Kraak ware. They were the *Witte Leeuw*, sunk in a fight with the Portuguese in the harbour at St Helena in 1613, and the *Banda*, wrecked off the coast of Mauritius in a storm in 1615.[42] An important study of the porcelain salvaged from the *Witte Leeuw* wreck site was published in 1982 by the Rijksmuseum in Amsterdam.

There is unfortunately no background of historical evidence to identify the Hatcher vessel or provide us with a date for the wreck, as there was for the *Witte Leeuw* and *Banda*. These two wreck sites were excavated under controlled conditions by marine archaeologists, whereas Captain Hatcher was carrying out a commercial salvage operation. Much valuable information has thereby been lost and many vital questions left unanswered, some of which were summarized in a recent review by Dr Oliver Impey, in which he concluded that it was 'certainly not an excavation upon which dating criteria can securely be based'.[43]

Dr Impey went on to describe our present knowledge of mid-seventeenth century porcelain as 'a muddle of half-resolved questions'. There is some truth in this, despite all the progress we have made in recent years, but Captain Hatcher has presented us with a magnificent opportunity to refine our knowledge. He has provided us, after all, with a documentary group of 25,000 pieces of porcelain, from which we can gain fresh insights into the rapid changes which were taking place in the middle years of the seventeenth century. It is unfortunate that our judgements will have to be made primarily on art historical rather than archaeological grounds, but this is hardly a new situation for students of Chinese ceramics. Our reconstruction of the history and development of Chinese porcelain depends largely on stylistic analysis and judgements based on familiarity with particular types of ware, with only a thin underpinning of what an archaeologist would regard as provable facts.

Let us begin by asking two basic questions: (1)how closely can we date the sinking of the vessel, and (2)are we justified in regarding all the 25,000 pieces as a newly made contemporary group?

Since they will inevitably be used as an important reference point for the dating of seventeenth-century porcelain, we need to form as precise a view as possible of when these wares were made and of whether earlier or later pieces are included among them. This is particularly necessary because there are groups of pieces which might well have been dated to the first quarter of the century if they had appeared individually on the market, and others which would probably have been described as Kangxi.

Both Colin Sheaf and Barbara Harrison suggested in their introductions to the sale catalogues that the making of the porcelain and the shipwreck took place within a few years of 1643. I am entirely in agreement with this view, but I should like to examine it in some detail and to suggest that there may be a mixture of historical and ceramic reasons for narrowing down the likely dates even further.

As regards the dating of the shipwreck, the strongest pieces of evidence are two covers for large oviform jars inscribed with cyclical dates. Both have the same seal mark and five-character inscription stating that they were written on a spring day in the *guiwei* year, equivalent to 1643 in the cyclical calendar (Pls. 12, 13).[44] If these two pieces had been recovered in the course of a controlled excavation, they

Pl. 12 (left). Barrel-shaped jar, with domed cover (Pl. 13, right), 26.5 cm ht. Inscription on cover dated to Spring 1643.

might have provided us with what archaeologists call a *terminus post quem*, a 'not earlier than' date for the event itself, the sinking of the ship. In other words, the wreck could not have occurred earlier than the spring of 1643, provided we accept that the inscriptions were indeed written at that time.[45] This logic would require the archaeologist to prove that the two jar covers could not be intrusive to the wreck, easier to establish in excavations on land, where stratigraphical techniques could be used, but difficult in an underwater site.

This reasoning would apply only to the sinking of the vessel, and could not necessarily be extended to the other porcelain, which might still have been made earlier or later than 1643: earlier because some or all of the porcelain might not have been newly made when the vessel sailed, and later because it would have been established only that the vessel sank 'not earlier than' 1643, with no implications as to how much *later* it might have sunk if the covers themselves were not new when they were shipped. There would thus be no restriction on a later manufacturing date for the rest of the porcelain.

I have quoted this piece of archaeological reasoning in order to give some idea of how much more we might have learned from a controlled excavation, and also to emphasize the essentially tentative nature of any conclusions we may reach concerning the dating of the Hatcher cargo.

So what conclusions can we – dare we – draw from the presence of the two dated jar covers? How else could they have come to be on the site if not as part of the Hatcher vessel's cargo? Could they have been thrown overboard from some other passing vessel, or could they have come from a second, undiscovered wreck on the same site? Before dismissing these possibilities, it should be remembered that later (and also possibly earlier) shards were recovered from the wreck site of the *Witte Leeuw*. However, the circumstances were rather different in that the *Witte Leeuw* was sunk while at anchor in the harbour at Jamestown, St Helena, a regular anchorage for vessels on their way home to Europe and a site where we might expect to find broken pieces of porcelain. Also the two jar covers were unbroken and therefore less likely, one would have thought, to have been thrown overboard. It is true that Captain Hatcher found the *Geldermalsen* on the same reef as the Hatcher junk, but the two wrecks were about a mile apart, and a second wreck on the same site, with the two cargoes intermingled, certainly seems a remote contingency.

We are surely entitled to conclude that the two jar covers are inherently more likely to have come from the Hatcher junk than from any other source. It can therefore be proposed that the wreck is *not likely* to have occurred earlier than the spring of 1643. Even without the covers, there were several other pieces of dating evidence among the porcelain. None would be considered conclusive in themselves, but taken together they draw us toward the same dates as the inscriptions on the covers have already indicated.

There were six dishes with the unusual decoration of a sea serpent reserved in white against a blue wave background. A dish in the Percival David Foundation with the same decoration has an inscription on the base reading 'fine vessel for the Kuangfu in the first year of Hongguang' (Pl. 14). Hongguang was the reign name taken by the Prince of Fu, who attempted to establish a Ming court at Nanjing in 1644–5, but was deposed after a few months.

The next Ming shadow emperor, Longwu, set himself up in Fujian province in 1645–6, but was also shortly overthrown. A pair of white-glazed joss-stick holders in the form of lion-dogs are illustrated by P. J. Donnelly, one of which is marked 'Longwu first year twelfth month, thirtieth day, a lucky day'.[46] There were several of these among the Hatcher cargo (Pl. 17), which Colin Sheaf described as being 'extremely close in both design and ceramic body' to the Donnelly pair.

Pl. 14. Dish dated 1644–5, 14.7 cm diam. *Percival David Foundation, London.*

There were also a number of mustard pots of the same shape as one sold at Sotheby's in May 1971 (Pl. 16), which has a 1643 cyclical date. The decoration of a scholar's table and a vase against a plain white background occurs on many Hatcher pieces, and will be shown below (page 47) to have been a popular contemporary motif which had recently been introduced.

It is interesting to compare the Hatcher wares with Dr T. Volker's extracts from the Dutch East India Company records of the period (see Appendix B). Orders were placed in 1643 and 1644, from which many of the more distinctive shapes can be identified among the Hatcher pieces. The closeness of this comparison is in itself rather convincing dating evidence, although it requires a year-by-year analysis of the expansion of the range of shapes ordered by the Dutch to illustrate the point.

Volker was careful to take note of new shapes as they appeared in the records. Two were first mentioned in 1643: one was an order for '1,000 nests of six small cups each', another 1,000 were ordered in 1644. There were two sets of these among the Hatcher finds (Pl. 15). Among the same two orders in 1643 and 1644, octagonal pots for preserves were listed for the first time. Octagonal pieces in other shapes had been popular for several years, but this was the first time that octagonal pots had been mentioned. The Hatcher cargo included 141 octagonal covered jars (Pl. 63). However, it should be pointed out that the records Volker referred to were far from complete. They are sufficient to show trends in the pattern of Dutch orders, but we could not conclude that any particular shape had definitely been first introduced at that date.

Pl. 15. Nest of six cups, 4.5–8 cm. diam. *Private collection.*

So we have several pieces of ceramic evidence referring us to the years 1643 to 1646. With these dates in mind, let us now look at the historical background and in particular at what happened to the porcelain trade.

The Manzus crossed the Great Wall and captured Beijing in June 1644, declaring the foundation of the Great Qing dynasty. They pursued the various Ming pretenders through Zhejiang, Fujian and Guangdong provinces, but did not succeed in establishing full control over these areas. The Manzus were horsemen rather than seafarers, and large areas of the southern coasts remained under the effective control of Ming loyalists for the next thirty-five years, until about 1680. They also retained control of the sea approaches and of seaborne trade.

As the Ming government collapsed, rebel bands roamed unchecked throughout the countryside. The Dutch received reports in January 1644 that the province where the porcelain was made was 'full of war', and in April of 'great mortality among the porcelain makers'.[47] The last order the Dutch were able to place was evidently in April 1644 for the huge total of 355,800 pieces, all intended for the European market.[48] Delivery to the Dutch trading post at Fort Zeelandia on Taiwan was expected in January 1645 and we know that at least part of this order was received, despite the turbulent condition of the country. However, the Manzus overran Jingdezhen in 1645, bringing export trade to a halt. Several shipments of porcelain were sent from Taiwan to Batavia in 1645 and 1646, the last being 72,258 pieces shipped in November 1646, which were probably a clearing-out of the last remnants held by the Dutch and by the Chinese merchants who supplied them.[49]

A small but illuminating incident is reported from Taiwan in March 1645. The Chinese merchants had brought some samples which were 'judged passable as to colour and design, but the dishes, especially the large ones, far too thick and heavy. This the Chinese had tried to excuse with fabricated reasons. They had alleged that these could not be made thinner and lighter because the clay was not suitable.'[50] This suggests that the merchants, no longer able to bring fine porcelain from Jingdezhen, had tried unsuccessfully to interest the Dutch in Swatow dishes,

Pl. 16. Mustard pot, 12.7 cm ht. Inscription dated to 1643. *Sold Sotheby's, London, 18 May 1971, Lot 222.*

Pl. 17. Pair of lion-dog joss-stick holders, 15 cm ht.

which were made at kilns near the coast in Fujian and northern Guangdong, areas still under the control of Ming loyalists. The Dutch were familiar with Swatow wares, selling them in large quantities in Asia, but the clay was not good enough quality to produce the fine porcelain required for the European market.

Occasional limited shipments are mentioned in the later 1640s and early 1650s, and Volker gives a latest date for shipment of fine Jingdezhen porcelain as 1657. However, although we should perhaps apply this as a safe terminal date for individual pieces of late Ming export ware, it seems unlikely from the historical evidence that the Hatcher group, covering such an extensive range of wares, including many types suitable only for export, could have been assembled for shipment later than the end of 1646.

The potters could of course have continued to make porcelain after 1645, but they were dependent for export orders on the merchants who financed the export trade and who would almost certainly have been associated with Ming loyalist factions in the coastal provinces. Even if the merchants were still able to travel to Jingdezhen or to send their orders, the Manzus were presumably preventing the free movement of trade goods to the coast. Smuggling such bulky and comparatively low-value goods would have been expensive and risky. Occasional batches of fine porcelain may have got through, but after 1645 it was clearly no longer commercially viable to order the special assortments, such as Kraak ware, for which there was no market in China.

The Hatcher vessel is therefore most likely to have been wrecked not earlier than 1643, on the evidence of the two dated jar covers, and not later than the end of 1646, if we may judge from the contemporary experience of the VOC. That being so, what conclusions can we draw concerning the dating of the porcelain? It would not be unusual for a batch of wares to have been in storage awaiting sale or shipment, although probably not for longer than a year or two in view of the very active market for porcelain at the time. We frequently find delivery or shipment delays occurring for a wide variety of reasons in the Dutch records.

Another way in which earlier pieces could have been introduced is as private cargo belonging to the crew, or to passengers or merchants travelling on board, of whom there were always many on Chinese junks sailing to South-East Asian ports. This would be one explanation for a number of apparently sixteenth-century shards retrieved from the site of the *Witte Leeuw* wreck.

This seems to be as far as a review of the circumstances surrounding the wreck can take us. To sum up, we have established a tentative date for the wreck itself as being between 1643 and 1646. However, part of the cargo might well have been made a year or two before the earliest date of the wreck, and we cannot exclude the possibility of still earlier pieces having been on board. Later pieces seem unlikely, even if we cannot entirely exclude the theoretical possibility. So the most probable dates for the manufacture of the porcelain are between 1640 and 1645.

Can we accept that all the tremendous variety of shapes and decorations are a contemporary or near-contemporary group of trade wares made between 1640 and 1645? This question should be kept in mind as we review the development and dating of Kraak and Transitional wares in relation to the Hatcher finds.

THE PORCELAIN

Approximately 25,000 pieces of unbroken porcelain were salvaged from the Hatcher junk. Those sold through the four sales at Christie's Amsterdam, totalling 22,178 pieces, are listed by shape and size in Appendix A. Captain Hatcher returned to the site in 1985 and salvaged over 2,000 more pieces, most of which were sold through a London dealer, Heirloom and Howard. Since they were not catalogued for auction, no individual descriptions are available, nor of groups of pieces dispersed by private sale and gifts to museums. The great majority of the 25,000 pieces were Jingdezhen blue and white, but there were also interesting groups of celadon, blanc-de-chine, coloured wares and provincial blue and white.

The overwhelming impression is of a tremendously wide range of shapes and designs. Over 200 shapes and sizes are listed in Appendix A, without any attempt to catalogue all the decorative motifs and border patterns. To take an example, there were a particularly attractive group of 227 blue and white tea pots, among which were sixteen shapes and no less than twenty-eight different decorations (Pl. 89). An entry in the Appendix such as '2,614 8.5/11 cm bowls' covers a wide range of small but possibly significant variations in the width of the foot, the height and angle of the side wall and the shaping of the rim.

Appendix B quotes a passage from Volker's translation of the VOC records for 1643, giving details of two typical orders placed with the Chinese merchants Jousit and Tecklim, as well as some interesting information about the beginnings of tea-drinking in Europe. Tecklim seems to have handled the Kraak orders, and Jousit those for the Transitional and other more recently introduced wares. It can be seen that the VOC were already ordering each item systematically in large quantities through their trading station on Taiwan. The Company's porcelain was frequently carried from Taiwan to Batavia in chartered Chinese junks rather than their own vessels. However, the diversified nature of the Hatcher load suggests that this was not a VOC cargo, but more probably a mixed consignment to be traded in the thriving wholesale markets at Batavia or Bantam.

The VOC did not hold any monopoly on the distribution of porcelain, even to Europe. The English were large, if irregular, buyers at Bantam for the European, Indian and Arab markets, while a steady stream of porcelain flowed to Holland as the private cargo of the Company's own employees. Indian and Middle Eastern merchants traded under safe-conduct passes issued by the Company, and South-

Pl. 18. An assorted group of pieces recovered when Captain Hatcher returned to the wreck site of the junk while searching for the *Geldermalsen.*

East Asian markets were served by private traders of many nationalities – Dutchmen who had left the service of the Company, Portuguese, Chinese who had settled abroad, and local rulers who controlled suitably located ports or areas producing pepper and other marketable commodities.

There were many shapes among the Hatcher wares that we should think of as being for the Chinese domestic market – incense burners, tripod bulb bowls, brush pots, bird feeders, cricket cages, garden seats and *zhadou.* Perhaps they were bringing the sophistications of life at home to the large and prosperous Chinese communities, or were intended simply to be sold as novelties. Ornamental items such as beaker vases, *rolwagens* and tall mallet-shaped or globular vases had originally been designed to decorate the Chinese scholar's study or the official's residence. The Dutch were also just beginning to appreciate these handsome pieces. An order was placed in 1644 and a shipment from Taiwan in 1645 included '1,205 flower pots among which large ones of beaker shape and round ones, half and quarter-sized ones of beaker shape, and round ones, "painted" ones and some

with handles'.[51] These are presumably *gu* beaker vases and *rolwagens*, 'painted'
meaning decorated with enamelled colours. Such large, impressive pieces, the less
familiar the better, also made excellent presents for local dignitaries. A report in
1649 from Wingurla, near Goa, advises that it was intended to present the King
with '20 large long-necked flasks of which 12 in a cabinet' and '2 large red-col-
oured *rolwagens* with leafwork in relief and flowers'.[52]

A division has previously been drawn between ornamental Transitional wares
for the domestic market and practical shapes for the Dutch dinner table.[53] This is
helpful for identifying the markets for which these wares were originally designed
in the 1630s, but it was becoming blurred in the 1640s as attractive and useful
shapes became popular in new markets. The mustard pot with a 1643 cyclical date
(Pl. 16) may be a case of a typically Dutch shape being put to some use in China,
since there would be no purpose in writing an inscription on a piece intended
exclusively for use by Dutchmen who could not read it. There was also a small
rolwagen among the Hatcher wares with the character '*you*' (oil) written in underglaze blue inside the rim (Pl. 68). The *rolwagen* derived from the traditional *meiping*
form, which had originally been a storage jar for liquids, but was used from late
Ming times as a vase to hold a branch of plum blossom.

The following sections will consider the Hatcher Kraak, Transitional, coloured
and provincial wares, and discuss what new insights they offer into the development of the various porcelain styles during the last decades of the Ming.

Kraak Ware

It used to be thought that the Kraak style died out at the end of the Wanli
period,[54] but it has been recognized in recent years that Kraak wares continued to
be made in vast quantities until the end of the Ming dynasty. The Hatcher finds
confirm this, provided we can satisfy ourselves that the Kraak wares among them
were not an earlier group which happened to be shipped on the Hatcher junk.

There were over 2,600 Kraak pieces recovered, including dishes, bowls, *klapmutsen*, flasks and *kendis*, but no cups. They are grouped separately under each
shape in Appendix A. The Hatcher pieces suggest that, although non-Kraak
designs were becoming popular for bowls, cups and flasks, the bulk of dishes for
export were still Kraak ware. Attractive new styles were emerging, particularly
for the smaller dishes and saucers, but there is no evidence that these were mass-
produced for export to compete with the established Kraak range of dishes.

A comparison between the wares salvaged from the *Witte Leeuw*, sunk in 1613,
and those recovered from the Hatcher junk shows that the panelled Kraak style
had changed remarkably little in thirty years. Plates 20–35 have been chosen to
illustrate the striking similarities in central subject, border designs, use of diapers
and overall arrangement on several different Kraak shapes.

Pl. 19. Barrel-shaped garden seat, with
moulded lion masks, 40.5 cm ht.

Pages 33–36: A comparison of Kraak
motifs on *Witte Leeuw* (left) and
Hatcher pieces. (*Witte Leeuw*
photographs courtesy of the Rijksmuseum,
Amsterdam).

Pls. 20 and 21 (top). Dishes with a bird
on a rock under a flowering peony,
28.7 and 47 cm diam.

Pls. 22 and 23 (centre). Dishes with
qilin, 50.1 and c.35 cm diam. Note the
fine lines on the *Witte Leeuw* piece, and
the thick outlining of the rocks. On
the Hatcher piece, the plain white
areas, the casual drawing of the diapers
and the 'tulips' are all later
characteristics.

Pls. 24 and 25 (bottom). Dishes with
flower basket, 32 and c.35 cm diam.
Note the V-shaped strokes on the
Hatcher piece to indicate grass.

Pls. 26 and 27. Dishes with grasshopper on a rock, c.30 and c.35 cm diam.

Pls. 28 and 29. Dishes with *meisande* (petalled) decoration of a bird on a rock, c.20 and c.14 cm diam.

Pls. 30 and 31. *Klapmutsen* with symbols, 22 and c.27 cm diam.

Pls. 32 and 33. Bowls with peony and insect panels, 13.2 and
c.11.5 cm diam.

Pls. 34 and 35. Pear-shaped flasks, 24.5 and c.27 cm ht.
The painting is simpler on both these pieces than on those above,
but the quick, casual brush strokes are very similar to each other.

Pls. 36 and 37. Betel boxes, oval and notched rectangular shapes,
c.11.5 and c.13–14 cm long.

Pls. 38 and 39. Dragon bowls, 14.2 and c.15 cm diam.
The blobby dot border on the inner rim of the Hatcher bowl is not
found on earlier wares.

Pls. 40 and 41. Cups, 4.9 and 4.7 cm diam.

There is also an interesting comparison in the size of dishes with flattened rim:

Witte Leeuw	*Hatcher*
49/52 cm. diam.	47/47.5 cm.
36.5	34.5/35.5
28.4/32	28.8/30
—	26/27.5
20.7/21.9	20/21
14.2	14/14.5

The *Witte Leeuw* dishes fall into five sizes. The Hatcher pieces still conform to these sizes, except that the largest platters have been reduced to 47 centimetres and there is one more intermediate size.

The Dutch habitually placed their orders in terms of 'full, half, third, quarter and eighth sizes', which must have represented dimensions understood by the Dutch, the Chinese traders with whom they dealt and the potters. Actual measurements are almost never stated in the VOC records, and it is likely that there was in fact no common standard of measurement understood by all parties.[55]

Another standardizing factor would have been the use of moulds. The dishes were thrown on a wheel and then pressed over a mould to produce the indented panels that are a characteristic of Kraak wares.[56] The potter therefore had to keep close to a standard size in order to fit the mould. The practice of using moulds dated back to the early days of Kraak ware in about the 1570s. The panelled style and some of the new shapes probably derived from Islamic pottery and metal ware sent by Portuguese or Moslem traders to be copied in porcelain, and the moulded panels may have been taken from metal ware. Almost all the *Witte Leeuw* Kraak wares were sharply moulded, but the practice seems to have been dying out and only a few of the larger Hatcher dishes have crude indentations, which look as if they were hastily made by hand by the potter himself. Otherwise, only some of the larger Hatcher *kendis* are moulded, and it may be that the lack of moulding can be taken as an indication of a later date.

Another interesting comparison is in the sizes of the *klapmutsen*, which were bowls with everted and flattened rims. They first appeared early in the century and seem to have been made specifically to Dutch order. The VOC ordered *klapmutsen* regularly, but always in only two sizes up to 1636, when they increased to three, and to four from 1637.[57] Since the *Witte Leeuw* pieces were 20 and 14 centimetres and the Hatcher ones 27 and 10 centimetres, we may have here the four sizes, implying that the largest and smallest were the ones added after 1636.

Despite their similarities to the *Witte Leeuw* pieces, the Hatcher Kraak wares have a number of features which distinguish them from earlier types and link them with the contemporary Transitional wares. The greyish and dark inky blues of the late Wanli period have been replaced by a more violet-toned blue. The potting tends to be heavier, without moulding, and covered with a thicker, slightly greenish glaze more akin to that found on Transitional pieces than the thin, glassy glaze on earlier Kraak wares. The designs are painted in a flatter, more two-dimensional style, with less use of dots and fine lines and more areas of pale wash. There is less attempt to fill every inch of the surface with decorative detail, leaving slightly larger areas of white around the painted designs in the Transitional manner, although they are still comparatively heavily decorated. Both groups show great variation in the quality of material used, and in the potting and painting technique, so that poor quality should not be taken in itself as an indication of later date. Many of these variations do not show up well in photographs and there is no substitute for handling the pieces themselves.

However, certain specifically Transitional features can be found. These include tulips (Pl. 23), the well-known V-shaped strokes (Pl. 25), vases and tables (Pl. 45, top left), and 'floating' flowers and insects (Pl. 45, top right). Note the deer with their noses in the air in Pl. 46 (top, second left), which are painted in a style quite different from early seventeenth-century Kraak wares. Also compare the 'sunflowers' in panels in Pls. 20 and 21; the single stem and flower are noticeably different from the Wanli version of this common motif. A further link with Transitional wares are the most unusual *kendis* with disc-shaped spout and neck. There are typically Kraak and Transitional versions (Pls. 49, 50), which must surely be contemporary.

It appears that certain Jingdezhen potteries specialized in Kraak wares for sixty or seventy years, continuing to turn them out year after year with few changes, simply because their overseas clients liked them as they were and few new designs came along to supplant them. Most of the stylistic developments in borders[58] and the use of diaper patterns seem to have taken place by or shortly after the turn of the century, with the exception of the limited Transitional influences referred to above. The *meisande*, or petalled, style (Pls. 28, 29) appears on a dish in a Dutch still-life painting by Nicholas Gillis dated 1601,[59] while the *klapmuts* is mentioned

Pl. 42. Gerrit Willemsz. Heda (c.1620–before 1702). Dutch still life. Compare with Kraak dishes, Pl. 45. 64.8 × 50.8 cm.

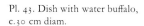

Pl. 43. Dish with water buffalo,
c. 30 cm diam.

in VOC records for the first time in 1608.[60] A covered high bowl similar to Pl. 54, complete with hare mark, was among the pieces in the Ardebil collection, which was not added to after 1607.[61]

There were 7,800 cups in a very wide range of shapes and decorations on the Hatcher junk, but no Kraak ones. The fashion for drinking tea and coffee had recently spread from the Middle East to Europe, and cups in new styles were in great demand. However, we cannot of course assume from their absence on the Hatcher junk that they were no longer being made, and it may equally well be that the demand for them continued to match the Kraak dishes, bowls and flasks on European dinner tables.

For students of Kraak ware anxious to date individual pieces as closely as possible, the *Witte Leeuw* and Hatcher finds have provided a quite unexpected bonanza of datable pieces for comparison. On the other hand, the continuation of basic shapes and designs over such a long period means that many of the more ordinary Kraak pieces will still be difficult to date.

As to whether there were earlier pieces included among the Hatcher Kraak wares, it certainly cannot be stated with any confidence that there were not. However, the evidence of Transitional influence and the many similarities which link them as a group make a 1640s date seem feasible. I have not been able to separate any pieces that do not fit in and might be suspected of being earlier, as there were on the *Witte Leeuw*.[62]

Perhaps not surprisingly, there were many other late Wanli and Tianqi types that seem to have continued to be made more or less unchanged. Again, comparisons can be made with pieces from the *Witte Leeuw* (Pl. 36–41). Other survivals of earlier styles are the traditional *guan* jars (Pl. 51), Red Cliffs bowls (Pl. 44),[63] lobed jars (Pl. 48) and dishes with net pattern (Pl. 55).[64]

Pl. 44. Bowl with scene and extract from the Song dynasty poem 'Ode to the Red Cliffs', 16.5 cm diam.

Pl. 45. Dishes, c.35 cm diam. Pear-shaped flasks, 27 cm ht.

Pl. 46. Dishes, c.27 cm diam. *Klapmutsen*, c.27 cm diam. *Kendis*,
20.5 cm ht.

Pl. 47. Dish with two deer, c.21 cm diam (centre). *Meisande* dish with horse above waves, c.14 cm diam (left). Shallow Transitional bowl, with hare and moon, 17.8 cm diam (right). Two Transitional bowls with phoenixes, c.11 cm diam (foreground).
The dish with the deer is a survival of an earlier, simpler style of Kraak decoration. There were similar pieces on the *Witte Leeuw*.

Pl. 48. (Top row) small *kendis*, c.13.5 cm ht; large bowl, c.36 cm diam. (Centre and bottom rows) *guan* jars with knobbed covers, c.24.5 cm ht; pear-shaped, onion-topped flasks, c.27 cm ht. Note the European flower ('tulip') decoration.

Pl. 49. *Kendi* with disc-shaped spout and top combined with Transitional decoration, 20 cm ht.
Pl. 50. (inset). Similar-shaped *kendi* but with Kraak decoration, c. 20 cm ht.

Pl. 51. Large *guan* jar, 40 cm ht.
Note the Transitional cartouches and 'floating' branches on what is otherwise a piece with Wanli
shape and decoration.

Pl. 52. Pair of dishes, 20.5 cm diam.
The perfunctory decoration on the underside is characteristic of Kraak ware of the very
late Ming. *Photo courtesy Julia Curtis.*

Pl. 53. A reticulated and an octagonal bowl, 9 cm diam.

Pl. 54. A pair of covered high bowls, with hare mark, 16.5 cm ht.
The hare mark is frequently found on later Wanli pieces, mainly jars, vases and flasks. It was probably the mark of a pottery or decorating workshop.

Pl. 55. Dishes with net pattern.

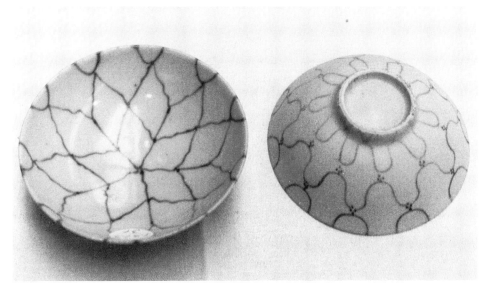

Ming Transitional Ware

In 1620, the eunuch Commissioner Pan Xiang, who had been responsible for the supply of porcelain to the Palace since 1599, was withdrawn after the death of the Emperor Wanli and not replaced.[65] No porcelain with the mark of the succeeding Tianqi period was found in the Palace, and there are almost no Tianqi marked pieces of Imperial quality known today.[66]

The organization of many of the better private potteries at Jingdezhen had revolved for generations around meeting the annual Imperial orders, so that the loss of patronage must have been a severe blow to them. Being accustomed to producing their wares in response to specific orders, either from the Palace or for export, the potters would have developed very little capacity to design, finance or market new products on their own initiative. Fortunately for them, overseas markets were thriving and there was a strong demand for a wider range and better quality of porcelain than the potteries making Kraak and the other established export types were able to meet.

However, it appears that at least one pottery specializing in hollow wares turned to the domestic market. Stephen Bushell, who visited Jingdezhen in the 1890s, mentions in his description of how the potteries were organized that there were 'three workshops for the making of vases (*cho ch'i*) fashioned on the wheel, including sacrificial vessels, jars and ornamental pieces of all kinds'.[67] It was evidently just such a workshop, or workshops, that began to produce the early Transitional types, mainly incense burners, vases, jars and brush pots.

The entire production process was clearly planned to set and maintain high standards. The materials were carefully prepared to produce a white, sturdy body and a thick, bubbly glaze that softened the appearance of the designs and would not chip at the edges. A good-quality cobalt[68] was refined to give a pleasing violet-toned blue that would not stand out too sharply against the plain white areas left undecorated. All these features appear for the first time on these beautiful new wares, although in due course they came to influence Kraak wares and other contemporary types.

The decorations were adapted from albums of woodblock prints and book illustrations. They include scenes from histories, mythical tales, popular novels, landscapes and studies of trees, flowers and birds. The introduction of woodblock printing had made it possible for art to be seen and enjoyed by a larger audience than the élite few able to own paintings and it was for this market, made up of the educated official and land-owning classes and the wealthy merchants, that the new wares were designed.

The central scene often occupies the whole surface of the pot without any secondary decoration at all, but delicately incised borders of waves and floral scrolls are sometimes used, enriching the decoration of the piece without complicating the uncluttered overall appearance. A spacious, airy feeling is created by leaving areas of plain white around the designs, which is in itself a departure from the heavily decorated Wanli Imperial and export wares. Borders of stiff vertical leaves may be used to emphasize the line of the foot or contrast with a gentle curve at the neck. Lappet, *ruyi* head and flame borders can also occasionally be found. In fact, these border patterns are the only feature carried over from Wanli wares.

The porcelain decorators faced the difficulty of transposing a picture designed to fit a flat, rectangular frame onto the round, often awkwardly shaped surface of the pots they were painting. A landscape or an elaborate scene with figures has its own perspectives and spatial relationships which, to be successful as a ceramic decoration, should not distract the eye from the essential lines and volumes of the pot itself. Thus, if a round pot is to be decorated with a scene of travellers in a landscape, it must be arranged as a pattern which will complement the curves and balance of the pot's shape from whichever side it is viewed, rather than drawing the eye immediately into the recesses of the scene depicted, as a painting might seek to do. One of the pleasures of Transitional wares is to see the various ways in which the decorators dealt with this basic problem.

In order to carry these elaborate decorations, a distinctive new range of wares was designed in which the emphasis seems to have been placed on finding the most basic geometric form for each ceramic shape, with straight or gently curving lines and as few angles as possible.[69] Individual shapes were drawn from very different sources. The *rolwagen* is a simplification of the traditional *meiping* vase; the brush pot is from bamboo; and the *gu* beaker vase, *gui* incense burner without handles, *zun* and *hu* vases are all new shapes in porcelain, derived from archaic bronzes.[70] The globular and barrel-shaped jars with domed covers, of which there are a number of variations, seem to have been mainly new designs, although possible antecedents can be found for some of them. The long-necked vases, too large and cumbersome to have a practical use as flasks, derive from smaller export

Pl. 56. Incense burner, with galloping horsemen, 17 cm diam. Inscription with cyclical date 1625. *British Museum, London.*

Pl. 57. Vase in the shape of a funerary urn, 46 cm ht. Inscription with cyclical date 1638. *British Museum, London.*

Pl. 58. Small barrel-shaped vase, 16.5 cm ht. Inscription with cyclical date 1636. *British Museum, London.*

Pl. 59. Barrel-shaped jar, cover missing, 16.5 cm ht. Inscription with cyclical date 1640. *Sold Christie's, London, February 1979, Lot 52.*

tablewares. Even the Transitional dishes and shallow bowls, which seem not to have appeared until the 1640s, may be seen in profile to have a regular, unbroken curve, as distinct from the standard saucer-dish shape with a flat well and curved or S-shaped sides.

We have no way of knowing when Transitional wares were first made, but three incense burners of unmistakable, if slightly coarse, Transitional type, with inscriptions dating them to 1625 and 1626 (see Appendix C), indicate that it was during the Tianqi period (1621–7). The presentation of pieces of porcelain to temples was an age-old custom, of which the David vases are a good example. Dedicatory inscriptions were often written on them, including the cyclical date and the name of the reigning Emperor.

There is then a gap, followed by a remarkable group of no less than twenty-two dated pieces falling into a ten-year period from 1634 to 1643. All are inscribed with a cyclical date, but only one has a reference to the reign or any other indication of which sixty-year cycle is referred to. This has given rise to doubts as to whether these pieces should not be dated sixty years later, but the recent publication of a typical Transitional bowl dated to the twelfth year of Chongzhen (1639)[71] and the evidence of the Hatcher wares should lead to general acceptance of a Ming date.

It was common practice to add cyclical dates to inscriptions on paintings, usually accompanied by lines of poetry appropriate to the picture, or a short dedication and the seal mark of the artist. This was taken up by the printmakers and the porcelain decorators followed suit, no doubt hoping to add a little *cachet* to their wares. Hence, we suddenly find quite a large group of pieces with this form of dating, which had only been used very occasionally on porcelain before this time and became increasingly infrequent thereafter.

A study group of twenty-two dated pieces enables us to look for developments and changes in the Transitional style. There are ten pieces, dated between 1634 and 1638, all in the pictorial style already described (Appendix C, nos. 4–13). Six of these are *rolwagens*, two are brush pots, one is a vase in the shape of a funerary urn (Pl. 57) and one is a small barrel-shaped vase (Pl. 58). Five have incised borders, which do not appear on any of the dated pieces after 1638, although it should be noted that they do appear on a Hatcher brush pot (Pls. 74, 75) and can occasionally be found on Shunzhi (1644–61) and early Kangxi wares, so that the practice did not die out altogether. Incised lines with no incised pattern are used on three other pieces dated to 1639 and 1640, and on many of the Hatcher Transitional wares.

From 1639, several new decorative arrangements begin to appear on the dated pieces. They recur constantly among the Hatcher wares. Cartouches in various shapes, including scrolls, leaves, peaches and fans, are used to limit the size of the main decoration. The earliest dated pieces are a 1640 jar (Pl. 59), a 1640 *rolwagen* in the Phoenix Art Museum and the 1643 Hatcher jar, which has a plain, rectangular cartouche (Pl. 12). The intention was probably to make the size of the scene more manageable for inexperienced decorators unable to cope with the problems of painting landscapes and figure scenes attractively on a larger scale.

There is also a variable arrangement of vases, scholars' tables, fishbowls and ornamental rocks (Pl. 68, left). It first appears on a 1639 beaker vase, the 1640 jar (Pl. 59) and the 1643 mustard pot referred to earlier (Pl. 16). This design should not be confused with the Wanli Flower Basket pattern, which still appears on Hatcher Kraak wares (Pl. 25). Another new motif which is particularly common among the Hatcher wares is of branches and floral sprays 'floating' on a plain white background (Pl. 63, top). It is used as the primary decoration on smaller pieces, or to fill in one area on larger pieces where the surface is divided into sections. The first time it appears is round the middle section of a 1640 beaker vase, on the 1640 Phoenix *rolwagen* and also on the neck of an enamelled *guan* jar in the Chicago Art Institute, dated to 1646.[72] It appears to derive from an earlier style with 'floating' flowers, insects and symbols, which can be found on pieces with Wanli and Tianqi marks and on a few Hatcher Kraak dishes and *guan* jars (Pl. 51).[73]

Pl. 60. Pear-shaped jug, with handle, 21.5 cm ht.
Note 'floating' flowers and branches.

As a measure of the change, one or other of these new designs appears on nine out of twelve of the pieces dated between 1639 and 1643, with only three continuing the early style. There are also occasional Hatcher Transitional pieces in the early style (Pl. 69) but most are in the new patterns, which we may take as being characteristic of the 1640s, although they were all to become absorbed into the Kangxi style.

The VOC records are full of complaints about the poor quality of the porcelain they were receiving. The Chinese merchants who travelled between Jingdezhen and the Dutch trading station on Taiwan with their annual porcelain orders must have seen the handsome new wares and brought samples to show the Dutch merchants. Hence the report from the chief merchant at Taiwan on 23 October 1635, which Volker paraphrases: '. . .the merchants have promised him on the strength of his promise to give a far better price for it, to bring with the next monsoon a good, fine assortment and that with this aim in view he has given them large dishes, large bowls, flasks, coolers, large pots, dinner dishes, beakers, salt-cellars, cups, mustard-pots and water-pots, and also flat dinner plates with broad rims and moreover wash-basins and their ewers, all made of wood, mostly turned, and painted with all kinds of Chinese figures which they have declared to be able to copy.'[74]

The wooden models are described as being 'painted with all kinds of Chinese figures', which certainly suggests that they had been copied from samples of Transitional wares. The shapes would not have been suitable for the Dutch market of the time, which would be the reason for models of standard tablewares being produced. Only hollow wares were being made in the Transitional style at this time, so that, while the Dutch were probably successful in obtaining such items as flasks, large pots, beakers and mustard pots, their orders for dishes, bowls and cups in the new style may not have been met for several more years. The Kraak potteries continued to dominate the market for flatwares, too set in their ways to adjust to the new designs beyond the inclusion of an occasional tulip or a figure scene in the centre of a large platter. But by the time the Hatcher wares were produced in the 1640s, a wider range of non-Kraak shapes was being made, mainly of small saucers, bowls and cups, which would not be described as Transitional, although many were broadly influenced by the Transitional style (Pls. 94 to 99).

Among the Hatcher pieces, Transitional tableware shapes made for the Dutch market include pear-shaped and double gourd flasks, drinking beakers, jugs and pear-shaped, globular and ribbed mustard pots. Ribbed shapes, including mustard pots, seem to have been a passing fashion which first appears in the VOC records in 1638. The covered jars were probably also made for the Dutch market. 'Pots for preserves' are first mentioned in 1635, 'very large fine covered pots' in 1636, and 'octagonal pots for preserves' in 1643. How they were used is indicated in a letter from Surat, dated 8 April 1637, requesting '16–18 porcelain jars of Radix China [a dried root used at the time as a medicine for skin disease], 20–25 with preserved ginger, 16–18 with pickled nuts, 2 with pickled cloves'.[75]

The decorations on the Dutch tablewares are in the same styles and give the impression of having been produced in the same potteries as the domestic wares. The only additions are painted, rather than incised, borders of flowers and scroll-

Pl. 61. Double gourd flask, with figures in landscape and 'tulips' on neck, 20 cm ht.

ing leaves. The tulip and other European flowers, which had been all the rage in the later 1630s, only survive on one Hatcher double gourd flask (Pl. 61) and on the largest Kraak dishes and bowls.

Thus far, there have been no real surprises among the Hatcher Transitional wares. The pieces we have considered can be accepted without any difficulty as having been made during the last decade of the Ming dynasty. However, there are a further group of pieces that would probably have been described as late Transitional or early Kangxi if they had appeared on the market as individual pieces. They are certainly unfamiliar in a Ming context, which has given rise to doubts whether the Hatcher wares are a contemporary group. These are the 'ginger jars', large covered boxes, miniature items, tea pots and the beautiful sets of dishes with overall pictorial designs in Transitional style. Let us consider each of these to see whether we can accept a Ming date for all of them, and to look at what links they have with the Transitional wares we have been discussing.

The 'ginger jar' (Pls. 63, 82) has always been thought of as a Kangxi shape,[76] although Arthur Spriggs drew attention to one in a painting by Willem Kalf dated 1658. The blue-washed, 'cracked ice' background pattern and the leaf-shaped cartouches in reserve are all new, but the central decorations of mythical animals and 'floating' flowers are commonly found on Hatcher Transitional and even Kraak wares, drawn in an identical way. The blue wash technique is used over a formalized wave pattern on several other shapes and on the 1645 David dish (Pl. 14).

Ewers with spout, handle and cover, for serving wines and sauces as well as tea,

Pl. 62. Dutch still life, attributed to Juriaan van Streek (c.1632–87). The painting shows a covered jar (compare Pl. 79) and a *klapmuts* (Pl. 30). 77.5 × 64.5 cm.

had long been established as porcelain articles in China. Two kinds were found on the *Witte Leeuw*, which would probably have been used for wine in Europe at that time, and a number of different types were exported to Japan for use in the tea ceremony. The only specific VOC orders were for '200 tea pots with covers and handles, also with ribs, according to No. 4 sample' in 1639 and '100 small tea kettles' in 1644.[77] These orders were signs of the growing cult of tea drinking (see Appendix B), of which the merchant whose cargo was being carried on the Hatcher junk was evidently well aware. Although there were a very wide range of shapes (Pl. 89), few had previously been thought of as Ming, but the decorations were mainly in the same styles as the other Hatcher Transitional wares. One particular type has an interior scene with figures on a chequered tile floor, most attractively painted in pale blue lines and washes. This is a new effect, but areas of pale blue are a feature of many Hatcher types. Pale blue is also strikingly used as a background in streaks (Pl. 63, middle left) and soft brush blobs (Pl. 83, top left) on other wares. The tea pots were a varied and charming new group, which must have been sent as samples to see which of the many styles would prove popular.

There were over 3,500 miniature items – small boxes, vases and jars in many different shapes (Pls. 84, 86, 87, 88). Such pieces had been popular exports to South-East Asia during the late Song and Yuan periods and they appeared again when the junk trade revived at the end of the fifteenth century. They continued to be in demand during this period, but the established market was for coarse wares. One would have thought these fine wares would have been too expensive to be sold in any numbers in Asian markets. There is no sign of such pieces among the VOC orders for Holland, so perhaps our enterprising merchant was hoping to create a new demand for them before events overtook him. Miniature items and tea pots became highly popular in Europe as soon as Chinese porcelain could be ordered again after 1680. The decorations include the now familiar cartouches enclosing sketchily painted landscapes in typical late Ming style, blue washes over waves and the use of V-shaped strokes.

There were twenty-three round and octagonal covered boxes, 18.5 to 23 centimetres in diameter, which were among the most finely decorated of all the Hatcher wares (Pls. 80 and 82). Plate 64 shows an octagonal box decorated in a pencilled style found on many of the group of wares we are now considering, but not previously associated with the Ming Transitional style. Various experiments had been made with pencilled drawing from the late Wanli period, but in noticeably different styles.[78] Perhaps we can detect here the beginnings of the stiffer, more mechanical Kangxi drawing. When looking at a Transitional piece, we are always aware of the hand and eye, and indeed often the limitations, of the individual decorator, but this sense of human contact tends to become lost in the impersonal precision of eighteenth-century brushwork. It is certainly a surprise to find that this stiffness had a Transitional origin, although it can be found in the drawing of other motifs once one looks for it. No doubt it was the inevitable result of commercial pressure to produce in large quantities and within a fixed time and price, which must have mounted as the demand for Transitional wares grew.

New border patterns of triangular, zigzag or wavy lines on this group of wares are not found on the earlier Transitional types.[79] They are often seen on the Shonzui wares made for the Japanese market, and suggest that these may also be dated to the last few years of the Ming. It is perhaps worth observing that several types of border often found on later Transitional wares datable to the 1660s and 1670s – pine needles, 'cracked ice' and blobby dots – do *not* appear, as borders at least, on Hatcher wares.[80] This also applies to the so-called 'Master of the Rocks' style of drawing.

We now come to the delightful sets of dishes decorated with landscapes or figure scenes covering the whole upper surface, without any border or other supporting decoration (Pl. 93). This style of decoration is really quite rare on Ming dishes, although it can occasionally be found on Wanli marked pieces and even on a type of hot-water bowl produced at the beginning of the sixteenth century.[81] It also appears on Tianqi dishes made for export to Japan,[82] which are in many ways the fore-runners of the early Transitional decorative style. The Hatcher dishes are so similar in design, material, sturdy potting and the simple unbroken curve of their shape as to suggest that the Transitional potteries, having begun with hollow wares, were now expanding their production. Compare the covered jar

Pl. 63. Three covered octagonal baluster jars (top), with 'floating' flowers and branches, c.35 cm ht. Below are six ovoid 'ginger jars', with drum-shaped covers, 28 and 32 cm ht.

Pl. 64. Octagonal covered box, with drawings of phoenixes, symbols, lotus flowers and tendrils in 'pencilled' style, 20 cm diam.

and two bowls with carved designs in Pl. 109, which must surely have been made at the same pottery. We may be tracing the development from a workshop specializing in hollow wares to a substantial commercial factory producing a widening range of wares in response to the growing popularity of the Transitional style both at home and abroad. There is, at present, no firm evidence to support this suggestion; what little we know of the organization and commercial background of the Jingdezhen potteries during this period was outlined above.

There were a dozen of these dishes 19.5 to 19.9 centimetres in diameter, decorated with illustrations from the novel *The Romance of the Three Kingdoms*, various scenes of figures in a garden or landscape setting, a Buddhist figure crossing the waves on a reed, and a landscape in the sparse style of the Yuan painter Ni Zan, whose work was a strong influence on the painters and printmakers of the Anhui school (Pl. 93, middle, second right).[83] Another eighteen saucer-dishes, 9 centimetres in diameter with foliated rims, also have figure scenes of Daoist immortals, ladies in gardens, travellers and warriors in landscape settings, as well as a pair with a squirrel and grape design; all with the unusual feature of a landscape across the underside viewed from one side only, rather than running around the dish (Pls. 96, 97).

Julia Curtis has some interesting comments on the decoration of these dishes in her article on the Hatcher wares in *Oriental Art*.[84] She draws attention to the four delightful snow scenes, in which pale blue washes have been most effectively used for contrast against a snowy landscape, with simple circles to suggest snow-laden branches (Pl. 65). These could probably be traced to a contemporary album of prints with studies of snow scenes.

Although they are clearly the work of the best decorators, there is nothing in the brushwork, decorative style, subject matter, tone of blue, potting, shape, glaze or body to cause us to doubt a 1640s date for these dishes. Indeed, if we take each

Pl. 65. Dish with cloaked figure riding through a snowy landscape, 19.6 cm diam.

of these features individually for the group of wares we are discussing, which might be suspected of being later, there is a strong web of similarities that weaves them together with the earlier Transitional wares, and even the Kraak wares, into what is surely a contemporary group.

Many of these comparisons are difficult to make from photographs. Sir Michael Butler has said that when he 'walked into Christie's huge room in March 1984 and saw the 8,000 or so pieces, it was *self-evident* that they were contemporary'.[85] The opportunity to form impressions by viewing the Hatcher wares *en masse* has now passed, but there are a number of museum and private collections that still enable comparisons to be made, and it is to be hoped that exhibitions will be mounted from time to time.

I have tried to look objectively at what clues we have towards the dating of the wreck, and at how earlier or later pieces of porcelain might theoretically have come to be salvaged from the wreck site. The possibility of earlier pieces cannot be excluded, at least in theory, although there do not seem to be any pieces among the Kraak or other potentially earlier types that do not fit in. The same exercise in searching among the later Transitional types has also not found any evidence which might lead us to suspect that a 1640s date cannot be applied to all the Hatcher wares. In any case, it is difficult to imagine how later undamaged pieces could have intruded onto a site in mid-ocean, as described by Captain Hatcher. We should have to suppose either a second wreck on exactly the same site, causing pieces to be intermingled in a way not detected by Hatcher, or a single wreck occurring later but which included a large consignment of pieces made in the 1640s. Without any supporting evidence, these alternatives must be regarded as less likely than the straightforward conclusion that these are a contemporary group of trade wares from a vessel that sank between 1643 and 1646. However, it should always be kept in the back of our minds that the argument rests on an accumulation of circumstantial evidence, ceramic comparisons and assessments of probability.

Nevertheless, it seems a reasonably secure base from which to view the Hatcher wares as a unique record of the porcelain being made at Jingdezhen at just the moment when the Ming dynasty came to an end. It becomes evident that the real difficulty has been to overcome preconceived ideas associating Kraak with Wanli, Transitional with the 1630s and 1640s, and 'ginger jars' and tea pots with Kangxi. The evidence that Kraak wares continued to be made until the end of the Ming dynasty and that the origins of the Kangxi decorative style were to be found in the Transitional wares has been accumulating for some years, but had still not prepared us for accepting that the enormous variety of shapes, designs and painting styles to be found among the Hatcher wares could all have flourished side by side at Jingdezhen. The Chongzhen period (1628–44) emerges as one of the most fertile in the history of Chinese porcelain, a remarkable reversal of the old view that it was an insignificant period during which no Imperial wares were produced.

The importance of the period is summed up by a perceptive comment I came across recently in a book by Ann Frank, in which she describes Kangxi porcelain as 'coasting on the momentum of innovation built up during the Transitional period'.[86] The Hatcher wares provide a remarkable demonstration of this point. It is also becoming clear that the famille verte style and palette, including the use of overglaze blue, as well as biscuit enamels and several monochrome glazes, all had their origin in late Ming times.

Pl. 67. *Rolwagen* (left) with deer and flying crane, 47.5 cm ht. Large double gourd vase (centre) with garden scene in fan-shaped cartouche, 36.5 cm ht. *Rolwagen* (right) with grazing horses in leaf-shaped cartouche, 44.5 cm ht.

Pl. 66 (left). Two *rolwagens*, one with a landscape and a bird on a branch in cartouches, the other with birds and flowering prunus branches, 47 and 48 cm ht.
A *rolwagen* in the Phoenix Museum with similar cartouches is dated 1640.

Pl. 68 (right). *Gu* beaker vase decorated with vases and scholars' tables (left) and *rolwagen* with the character '*you*' ('oil') written inside the rim, both c.22 cm ht.

Pl. 69 (far right). Brush pot, with figures in a landscape, 16 cm ht.

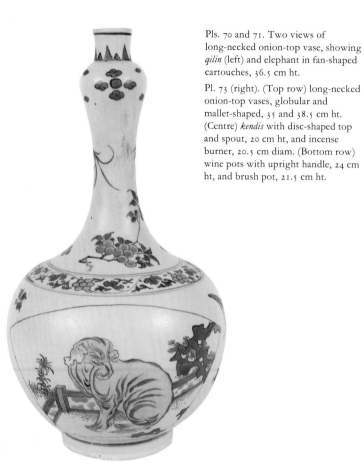

Pls. 70 and 71. Two views of long-necked onion-top vase, showing *qilin* (left) and elephant in fan-shaped cartouches, 36.5 cm ht.

Pl. 73 (right). (Top row) long-necked onion-top vases, globular and mallet-shaped, 35 and 38.5 cm ht. (Centre) *kendis* with disc-shaped top and spout, 20 cm ht, and incense burner, 20.5 cm diam. (Bottom row) wine pots with upright handle, 24 cm ht, and brush pot, 21.5 cm ht.

Pl. 72. (Top row) long-necked onion-top vases, globular and mallet-shaped, 36–8 cm ht. (Bottom row) pear-shaped and double gourd flasks, *gu* beaker vases and a *rolwagen*, 20–22 cm ht.

Pls. 74 and 75 (right). Two views of the same brush pot, with landscape in the style of Nizan and incised border, 19.5 cm ht.

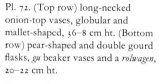

Pl. 76 (above). (Top row) two mustard pots with handles, one with cover, 12.5 and 11.7 cm ht; two small barrel-shaped covered jars, 10 cm ht; two covered bowls, with floral designs. 7.5 cm ht. (Bottom row) two drinking beakers, c.18 cm ht (this shape derives from European beakers in silver or pewter); two jarlets, with narrow neck, 9.7 cm ht; two covered bowls, decorated with vases and scholars' tables, 10.5 cm ht; two small covered jars, with notched rim for spoon, c.6 cm ht; two small cylindrical covered boxes, 4.7 cm diam.

Pl. 77 (left). (Top to bottom) two *rolwagens*, with tall narrow necks, 47.5 and 49.5 cm ht; three covered baluster jars, c. 33 cm ht; three covered boxes, 22 cm diam.

Pl. 78. Two covered jars, compressed globular, with metal knobs and handles, 21 and 22 cm
ht. One (left) is decorated with a *qilin* and phoenix, the other with a landscape.

Pl. 79. (Top row) two covered jars, slender ovoid shape, with domed cover, 20 cm ht; two
jars, with lobed rounded sides, 12 and 12.5 cm ht; covered jar, compressed globular shape,
metal knob and handles, 18.5 cm ht. (Bottom row) three bowls, with landscapes and
Buddhist wheel symbols, 16 and 20.5 cm diam; two brush pots, with landscapes in
cartouches, 15 cm ht.

Pl. 80. Compressed globular covered box, with phoenixes among flower scrolls, 21 cm diam.

Pl. 81 (right). Double gourd flask, with cloud collars enclosing lotus flowers reserved in white, 13. cm ht.

Pl. 82 (below). Five barrel-shaped 'ginger jars', with drum-shaped covers, 18–20 cm ht; three covered boxes, compressed globular shape, 20–21 cm diam.

Pl. 84. Eight covered boxes, four compressed globular shape, four cylindrical, c.4–5 cm diam.

Pl. 83. Six covered boxes, compressed globular shape, c.9 cm diam.

Pl. 85 (right). Three covered boxes, compressed globular shape, with pierced liners, 8–9 cm diam. Two have pencilled drawings of phoenixes, the third a landscape in a square cartouche.

Pl. 86. A group of twenty-one miniature vases of various shapes, c.6.5 cm ht.

Pl. 87. Eight miniature vases, in elongated and pear-shaped forms, with wispy
plants, c.12.5 cm ht; four cups with dragons in clouds, 4.3 cm ht; two covered
boxes, compressed globular shape, with pencilled flowers and scrolling leaves,
c.9 cm diam.

Pl. 88. Fourteen covered jarlets, with notch for spoon, c.6 cm ht.

Pl. 89. Twelve tea pots in various new shapes not previously seen in Ming wares,
9–17 cm ht.

Pl. 90 (left). Two tea pots, one barrel-shaped, the other hexagonal, 19 and 12.3 cm ht.

Pl. 91 (below left). Cadogan wine pot, peach-shaped, 15 cm ht.
The wine is poured into a hole in the base through a tube rising to near the top, so that no stopper is needed.

Pl. 92 (right). Two tea pots, with figures in landscape, c.13.5 cm ht.

Pl. 93 (below). Twelve dishes, with overall designs of landscapes and scenes with figures, 19.5–19.9 cm diam.

Pl. 95 (above). Two saucer-dishes, foliate rims, with a sea monster reserved in white against a blue wave background, Jiajing mark, c.14 cm diam.

Pl. 94 (left). Eight saucer-dishes, with straight and foliate rims, 8.5–9 cm diam.

Pl. 96 (above). Underside of saucer-dish similar to those illustrated right, Jiajing mark, 9 cm diam.

Pl. 97 (right). Six saucer-dishes, foliate rims, 9 cm diam.

Pl. 98. Eight cups and small bowls, c.6–11 cm diam.

Pl. 99 (below). Nine cups and small bowls, 6.5–8.5 cm diam; brush washer with inturned mouth, 8 cm diam.

Pl. 100 (bottom). Three tall cups, with erotic scenes, 7 cm ht.

Pl. 101 (above). Two spouted and two baluster flat-backed wall vases, 18.7 and 11.7 cm ht.

Pl. 102 (above). Covered bowl, with landscapes, 12 cm ht.

Pl. 103 (right). Large bowl, with birds flying among trees and rocks, Jiajing mark, 20.4 cm diam.

Pl. 104. Two covered bowls, with pencilled phoenixes and symbols, 10.5 cm ht.

Pl. 105. Bowl with knobbed cover, with orchids and other flowering plants in underglaze blue and brown (copper red?), c.15.5 cm ht.

Pl. 106. Pair of large bowls, everted rims, with phoenixes in the centre, tightly scrolling leaves on the cavetto and medallions on the outside, Jiajing mark, 20.7 cm diam.

Pl. 107. Two bird feeders, with lotus scrolls in pencilled style, Xuande mark, 6 cm diam.

Pl. 108. Small rectangular tray, with a galloping horse reserved in white under a blue wash, 9 cm long.

Pl. 109. Two large bowls and a covered jar, with carved flowers, 18.5 cm diam (bowls), 19.5 cm ht (jar).

Pl. 110 (opposite page, top). (Top row, left to right) two reticulated octagonal bowls, 11 cm diam; six octagonal bowls, 12 cm diam; two reticulated round bowls, 10.5 cm diam. (Bottom row) two ribbed mustard pots, covers missing, 11.5 cm ht; seven octagonal bowls, 9 cm diam; bowl, with foliate-tailed dragon, 11 cm diam; six bowls, decorated with horses galloping above waves, 9 cm diam.

Pl. 111 (opposite page, below). Cat nightlight on stand, the eyes and mouth pierced to show the light from a candle placed inside to frighten mice, 13 cm long.

Blanc-de-Chine

P.J. Donnelly's study of blanc-de-chine wares, published in 1969, is still the definitive work on the subject. He discussed and illustrated a number of pieces dated to the sixteenth and early seventeenth centuries, including the 1645 Buddhist lion joss-stick holder referred to above (see page 27). However, he went on to conclude that 'the kilns reached the zenith of their artistic creation and output in the fifty years or so corresponding roughly to the last quarter of the seventeenth century and the first quarter of the eighteenth' and to place the bulk of the wares into the Kangxi period.[88] His lead has been widely and no doubt in the main quite correctly followed, but the Hatcher wares do indicate that a substantial range of shapes were already being produced for export by the end of the Ming. The shapes show the same simple, elegant lines and interest in reproducing archaic bronze forms seen in the Transitional blue and white wares, reflecting the scholarly tastes of the period.

A total of 579 blanc-de-chine wares were sold in the Christie's sales, of which 439 were bowls in nests of five or moulded in the shape of flower heads. The other shapes and sizes are listed in Appendix A. Another 266 pieces were sold through Heirloom and Howard. They include 83 small wine cups and about 100 covered boxes in three sizes, 14, 10 and 6 centimetres, with ribbed sides and moulded floral patterns on the covers.[89]

Pl. 112. Three blanc-de-chine figures of Guanyin. *Private collection, Singapore.*

Pl. 113. A group of blanc-de-chine wares. (Top row) two cylindrical incense burners, 11.3 cm diam, and saucer-dish, 11.5 cm diam. (Middle row, left to right) water dropper in the shape of a boy holding a lotus spray, 11 cm ht; surprise cup, with moulded figure, 7.5 cm diam; brush pot, with carved leaf design and bands of incised scrolls, 19.5 cm diam; cup in the form of a lychee, 8.5 cm long; water dropper in the form of a figure riding on a fish, 9.5 cm ht. (Bottom row) tea pot, 10 cm ht; cylindrical incense brner, 8.2 cm diam; *gu* beaker vase, with protruding central bead, 21 cm ht: stem cup, 6.6 cm ht; wine pot, in the form of a section of bamboo, with animal spout and handle, 15 cm ht.

Celadon

Celadon wares had been produced at the Longquan kilns in the south-west of Zhejiang province from Southern Song times. They were established export items to the Middle East, India and South-East Asia during the thirteenth, fourteenth and fifteenth centuries, but were eclipsed by the popularity of the Jingdezhen blue and white wares. Various celadon-glazed wares were also produced for export at other kilns in Fujian and elsewhere.[90]

When they first arrived in the East in about 1600, the Dutch reported home that *gory* (celadon) dishes were in demand for Golconda in India. There is then no further mention until 1641, when twenty-one *gory* dishes are recorded as being in stock at Pulicat. In 1646, perhaps as a result of the shortage of blue and white, there are references to 1,176 *gory* dishes in Masulipatam, 2,000 being ordered from Mocha (near the modern Aden) and 1,000 from Coromandel. There are further scattered references during the next two decades, including an interesting gift in 1652 by a Dutch ambassador to the Persian Court of Shah Abbas II of '6 veritable antique *gouris*'. They are valued at 73 florins each, whereas the normal celadon dishes were worth less than 1 florin.[91]

There were a total of 396 celadons listed in the Christie's catalogues and among the pieces sold through Heirloom and Howard. The dishes, saucers and bowls were plain and ribbed, with straight and foliate rims, some with incised designs. The dishes were in four size groups ranging from 20 to 37.5 centimetres diameter. There were three bowl sizes from 13 to 23 centimetres diameter, as well as saucers, jars and small circular covered boxes. The glaze colour was described as 'medium olive-green to faded grey-green'.[92]

Pl. 114. Celadon dish with incised central pattern and border, 36 cm diam.

Pl. 115. A group of celadons of various colours, c.30, 20 and 13 cm diam, jarlet 6.5 cm ht.
The largest dish originally had an overglaze decoration in red and green enamels in typical Swatow style. The silvery traces of a *qilin* can be seen in the centre. The enamels had been eroded by long immersion in salt water, but the patches of red and green near the top were hidden under a large shell which had attached itself to the dish. *Heirloom and Howard, London.*

Pl. 116. Brown-glazed Swatow dish, with dragon design in white slip, 35 cm diam.

Provincial Blue and White

Coarse blue and white wares began to be made in the coastal regions of Fujian and Guangdong provinces during the second half of the sixteenth century. These kilns were meeting a demand in South-East Asia for dishes and rice bowls, which had previously been supplied by potteries in the vicinity of Jingdezhen. They had closed down as skilled labour was drawn into Jingdezhen itself to work at the growing number of potteries producing fine porcelain for the Court and for export.

Best known are the Swatow wares, which were coarse and presumably cheaper versions of early sixteenth-century and Kraak large dishes and bowls. However, 'Swatow' is used as a generic term for provincial late Ming export wares which were no doubt made in many small kilns up and down the coast. I used to live near the village of Wan Yiu in the New Territories of Hong Kong, where there is a kiln site said to have operated from the Ming period until the turn of the last century.[87] The site has not been excavated, but there are kiln wasters of bowls and dishes similar to some of those recovered from the Hatcher junk and the *Geldermalsen*.

It is often difficult to be sure even in which century these coarse wares were made, so that being able to associate specific pieces with a datable event such as a shipwreck is a valuable start towards establishing a chronology for them. This will be particularly helpful to archaeologists in South-East Asia, where shards of pottery and coins are often the only datable objects found. About 300 pieces were sold through Heirloom and Howard; a representative group is shown in Pl. 117.

Pl. 117. Three provincial bowls and a dish, with phoenix pattern. *Heirloom and Howard, London.*

Coloured Wares

Blue is the monochrome colour most often seen on the Hatcher wares, but we should distinguish between pieces with a blue glaze and those on which a wash of underglaze blue is used under a clear glaze. The latter is really an extension of the underglaze-blue decorating technique. As we saw in the section on Transitional wares, the decorators had been experimenting with light and dark washes and soft brush effects in a number of ways. For instance, an unusual effect was created by drawing in dark blue pencilled lines under a pale blue wash (Pl. 108). There were about 1,000 blue-washed pieces in quite a wide variety of shapes, listed separately under each shape in Appendix A. The use of a blue glaze produces a darker, thicker blue suitable for larger pieces. It is found on about 150 dishes and bowls among the Hatcher wares.[93]

A group of small round and octagonal covered boxes were sold through Heirloom and Howard. Most had a dark green or occasionally an eggyolk-yellow glaze, but some had been covered with what appeared to be a thin layer of red lacquer on which there were signs of drawing in gilt (Pl. 118). The second Christie's sale also included single items in various shades of green, yellow, brown and cream glazes.[94]

Pl. 116 shows a large brown-glazed Swatow dish, boldly decorated in white slip. This was a popular seventeenth-century type made for export to South-East Asia. The technique of decorating in white slip over a blue or brown glaze was also used at Jingdezhen during the sixteenth century and pieces with Wanli marks are known.[95]

The only polychrome wares were a delightful lotus bud cup, four brinjal bowls[96] and three cricket cages or potpourris, decorated on the biscuit in green and aubergine enamels on a soft yellow ground. Painting on the biscuit is yet another technique which has been thought of as a Kangxi rather than a Ming innovation.

As we found at the end of the section on blue and white Transitional wares, and with blanc-de-chine, the enormous output of the Jingdezhen potteries after 1683, when Imperial supervision was restored and large-scale exports to Europe were able to resume, has misled us into attributing many styles and techniques to the Kangxi period which had in fact begun to develop several decades earlier. There were already a number of individual indications of this from contemporary records and datable pieces, for which the Hatcher wares have now provided a focal point, enabling us to assess the level of ceramic development reached as the Ming dynasty came to an end.

The period from 1645 to 1683 was one of severely reduced output at Jingdezhen, with export markets cut off by the political situation and no regular orders from the Palace. Nevertheless, styles continued to change and a new refinement is evident in the potting and brushwork on a group of dishes cyclically dated to around 1670.[97] Sir Michael Butler has done much to identify the wares of this neglected period,[98] and the way is now open for a reassessment of the Kangxi period itself. Perhaps Captain Hatcher can oblige with a third wreck, this time datable to about 1690!

Pl. 118 (above). A group of enamelled covered boxes: (top left) two boxes with dark green lead glaze, moulded characters on the covers, one with a fitted bronze mirror, c.7 cm diam; two smaller boxes with dark green glaze, moulded honeycomb design, one without cover, c.4 cm diam; covered box in red lacquer, traces of gilt drawing, c.4.5 cm diam; base of box with yellow lead glaze, moulded honeycomb design, c.4 cm diam. *Heirloom and Howard, London.*

Pl. 119 (left). Flower-shaped water dropper, with spout in the stalk, pale green and traces of yellow wash on the biscuit. *Private collection, Singapore.*

Pl. 120. Blue-glazed and blue-washed decoration. The two saucer-dishes, 19.5 cm diam (top left and right), four large bowls, 21 and 18.5 cm diam (top centre and bottom) and the outside of the two small bowls, 9 cm diam, are all blue-glazed. The other pieces, apart from the three bell-shaped cups, have a wash of pale blue, sometimes over a darker blue fish-scale or dragon design, under a clear glaze.

THE GELDERMALSEN (1752)

EARLY WESTERN TRADERS AND EXPORT CERAMICS

During most of the sixteenth century, the trade with the Far East – spasmodic as it was – was a virtual monopoly of the major Catholic nations Portugal and Spain. Their supremacy at sea derived from the vast riches in bullion and precious stones shipped annually from the territories conquered or colonized in the New World, India and the Philippines. Spanish galleons and Portuguese carracks, the massive, heavily armoured lumbering giants of sixteenth-century maritime history, dominated the lucrative routes worldwide, bringing back all manner of exotic merchandise and precious commodities, including export-quality blue and white porcelain, to Lisbon, Cadiz and ultimately to Antwerp. On the rare occasions that a galleon was seized, as in 1602 and 1603, the Chinese porcelain auctioned off in Europe from the cargo of these 'prizes' attracted enormous interest.

The broader-based interest in Chinese porcelain which this increased availability engendered among the richer groups in European society in the early seventeenth century led to a largely uneventful annual business importing functional Chinese ceramics for domestic use; the trade in which the *Geldermalsen* (among many other ships) was routinely involved in the middle of the eighteenth century.

The Catholic sea-going armoured trading vessels were much feared by their Protestant rivals, but they were not invulnerable. Improved metal-casting technology in Elizabethan England and Continental Europe meant that more powerful, more reliable cannon could be cast in iron and bronze, which greatly diminished the relative naval supremacy of the larger but slower ships. The Protestant powers could clearly see the great profits to be made from directly trading with both Indies themselves, rather than relying on the Iberian entrepot trade (primarily through Lisbon) to make available the spices and sumptuous textiles which were the envy of all civilized societies in late Renaissance Europe. It was no accident that the earliest systematic Dutch voyages came at the time the Spanish monarchy established what was to be a sixty-year sovereignty over their long-time rivals, the Portuguese. The amalgamation of the two Crowns in 1580 led to the blockading, and closure, of Lisbon as the entrepot for oriental goods in Europe.

Pl. 121. Porcelain and gold from the *Geldermalsen,* still widely known to the public as the 'Nanking Cargo'.

Pl. 122. Peter Monamy (1689-1749).
An English three-decker with the
Union flag at the main as
Commander-in-chief, engaging a
Dutch admiral. 96.5 × 121.9 cm.

After the closure of Lisbon, the Dutch were both forced and encouraged to
undertake these long, arduous and uncertain voyages direct to the East themselves, in sturdy little boats, part military, part mercantile. Their increasing confidence to flout the *de facto* maritime monopolies of the Catholic powers worldwide
gave rise to the first great Western trading empire in the Far East, after the successful conclusion to the Netherlands War of Independence.[1] The Netherlands
secured independence from Spanish Hapsburg rule, and the subsequent growth of
Amsterdam (at the expense of Antwerp) made it Europe's major centre for the
great bulk shipping trades: corn and timber southward, fish and salt northward.[2]

The history of Western trade in the Far East during the seventeenth and eighteenth centuries developed entirely from changes within Europe (Pl. 122). It was
initially a series of struggles – which the Dutch primarily won – to take over or
establish fortified trading posts ('factories'), to protect valuable sources of local
products, and to disrupt wherever possible the trading arrangements of Western
competitors.[3] In 1602, six Dutch provinces acquired a corporate charter to trade as
a monopoly company in Far Eastern waters; their initiative was mirrored by one
from the English 'London East India Company', chartered to the same effect, and
immediately the territorial rivalry began. The Dutch were in Java from 1610, at
Bantam in the north-west. British pressure in the entrepot there prompted the
Dutch to move their factory ten miles eastwards, in 1621, and from then on the
entrepot at Batavia was their most important foothold in the East.

Western trade in the Far East at this period was essentially haphazard, as were
decisions concerning the acquisition of territories and the establishment of new
'factories'. The vital consideration was to end up with a substantial book profit.
Captains and business managers had great flexibility in the trading decisions they
made in the course of a typically rambling one- or two-year sojourn in the East,
selling or bartering the changing elements of the cargo a dozen times, in different
entrepots and 'factories'. They might be censured eventually by the Company they

represented, but it seemed impossible for Western committees to exercise more than the most general control over a voyage. The first Western merchants were not initially carving out new patterns of trade with the East. They were simply insinuating themselves into a long-established, complex and lucrative system, wherever they could find an opening.

Such haphazard trading, and the shifting nature of political allegiances made with local rulers as their ability to provide goods and services waxed or waned, made it essential to have a very detailed knowledge of trading circumstances in the East. How crucial this was is illustrated by the accidental survival in Vienna of one of the most remarkable records of Western overseas trade in the seventeenth century, compiled c. 1662–78. It is the 'Secret Atlas' of the Dutch East India Company, included as part of a collection (for the Company archives) of as many charts, maps and unpublished documents as the famous Dutch cartographer J. Blaeu (1596–1673) could assemble. So secret and important a trading asset was knowledge of the more productive islands of the Malaysian archipelago and the South China Seas that the existence of this particular volume within Blaeu's vast compilation is known only from one extant, illegally produced copy; the original Dutch archive copy has disappeared.[4]

From the earliest days, the Dutch had in theory a tight organization to control their trading activities overseas (Pls. 124, 125). The huge distances involved in transmitting instructions meant that it was vital to have an efficient local council, overseen in general terms by the administration in the Netherlands. The central body set up to initiate and run Dutch overseas trade was chartered by the States General of the Netherlands in 1602, and officially entitled the 'Verenigde Ooost-Indische Compagnie' (VOC).[5] The monopoly trading rights granted extended from east of the Cape of Good Hope right to the Magellan Straits. Its governing structure at home was two-fold. The lower tier was the Grand Council of sixty

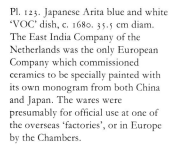

Pl. 123. Japanese Arita blue and white 'VOC' dish, c. 1680. 35.5 cm diam. The East India Company of the Netherlands was the only European Company which commissioned ceramics to be specially painted with its own monogram from both China and Japan. The wares were presumably for official use at one of the overseas 'factories', or in Europe by the Chambers.

representatives, elected annually from the geographical areas (the Dutch called them 'Chambers') which provided the operating capital for the Company. Initially there were six Chambers participating in the administration of the VOC, representing Amsterdam, Zeeland, Delft, Hoorn, Rotterdam and Enkhuizen; by the mid-eighteenth century, the major factories at Surat and Batavia had also been incorporated as Chambers. Each of these at the beginning was entitled to appoint representatives to the Executive Council, the 'Seventeen Gentlemen' ('Heren XVII'). This higher council was structured in such a way that no single Chamber could dominate strategic or financial decision-making by virtue of a numerical majority. This safeguard was in practice rendered less effective by Amsterdam's *de facto* grip on the Council. As the most influential Chamber, Amsterdam was entitled to provide four delegates right from the inception of the Heren XVII; Zeeland sent three, and the others sent one each.[6] This left one seat which was circulated every year to a different Chamber. The central Executive Council, through a number of sub-committees, decided the strategy for territorial expansion, supervised the commissioning of ships, appointed captains and business agents, gave instructions for the purchase (and subsequent auction sale) of goods from every factory, and analysed in great depth the annual trading figures on which most of the strategic decisions were based.[7]

Pl. 124. Famille rose plate for the Dutch East India Company, c.1730. 23 cm diam.
The design reproduces closely that on the new Company coinage specially commissioned for commercial use in the Dutch East Indies and introduced in 1728. A decorator in China, almost certainly at Canton, must have had one of these ducatoon coins available to copy very soon after this date.

From its headquarters at Batavia in Java, and the anchorage called 'Batavia Roads', the Dutch came increasingly to dominate the sea routes to Europe during the seventeenth century. The 'factory' at Batavia was administered by the 'Hoge Regering', the most elevated level of local council that the VOC created within its trading empire; smaller factories like Fort Zeelandia, Deshima and (later) Canton took instructions from the Hoge Regering, but were also subject to direct control from the Heren XVII. This organizational structure gave rise to hostile and acerbic correspondence between the Netherlands and Batavia; the latter consistently sought to preserve a prickly autonomy, and for nearly a century the VOC trade with China was a source of great friction as both the Heren XVII and the Hoge Regering tried to keep its direction under their respective control.[8]

The great value of Batavia for the Dutch lay in its relative closeness to the Chinese mainland. The Chinese junk trade with Western 'factories' in South-East Asia was long established.[9] Chinese junks from Zhangzhou had long supplied the Spanish at Luzon in the Philippines with goods, including some of the earliest Chinese export ivory carvings, the shapes themselves based on imported Catholic religious sculpture.[10] Meanwhile, the Portuguese first began to infiltrate the South Asian trading networks by displacing local junks from the lucrative carrying trade they had previously enjoyed between Japan and China.[11]

By the middle of the eighteenth century, the haphazard nature of Western trade with China had largely altered, although it was still predominantly in Protestant hands. Trade with the Far East – and most especially China – had turned into a much more carefully co-ordinated, regular and administratively uneventful annual event; although with uncertain weather patterns, incomplete charts and serious risk of piracy, it was still hazardous. The critical change had been engineered by the Chinese themselves, with twin objectives: a financial one, to gather rather more import and export duty, and a judicial one, to provide less opportunity for Westerners to antagonize or disrupt local communities (which had long been a problem when crews got ashore). From these requirements evolved what has become known as the 'Canton System', whereby the Chinese compelled (not entirely successfully) Western merchants to trade as far as possible only with a group of designated Chinese merchant-financiers, all based in the city-port of Canton, capital of Guangdong province on the coast of south-east China. It was, for the Chinese, one prong of an administrative reform to make revenue collection from all overseas trade more convenient; the other prong was to reserve Ningbe and Chusan for Korean and Japanese trading junks.

Western traders had seemingly regarded Canton during the seventeenth century in much the same light as other trading ports along the coast of the mainland; Amoy, Ningbe, and latterly Chusan (convenient for the Japan trade).[12] By the mid-eighteenth century the Chinese were turning the screw. In 1757, supercargoes reported to London that very little porcelain was available at one traditional hunting ground, Chusan. (Despite Chinese bureaucratic endeavours, it is interesting that they were still able and prepared to reach there, a long way north.) They go on to note that a Chinese official enquired 'what can be the reason of any of our ships coming to Lingpo in preference to Canton, which is the proper port for the European trade and where all our goods care to be acquired so easily. As Lingpo is solely for vessels which come from Japan and Corea. He thinks it also unreasonable for us to expect to have liberty to Trade where we please, when we permit the Chinese junks to go only to Batavia and Burnio'. The Batavian stranglehold on the Chinese junk trade may have seemed as burdensome to the Chinese as the Canton System did to Western merchants.[13]

This evolving system institutionalized Western trade with China. It gave the Chinese authorities at Canton, officials of the provincial Viceroy, the whiphand in every negotiation, every revenue problem and every question of what to trade. The Chinese laid down what they wanted imported as commodities to buy, they specified the laws to which the Canton expatriate community was subject, and they nominated the local merchant intermediaries, through whom all Western trade was to flow. This body of local merchants, formed officially in 1720 but only revived in 1759, was called the 'Co-Hong'; flexible in numbers, its membership fluctuated between about twelve and twenty accredited merchants, who did their best to prevent supercargoes trading outside their circle. As individuals, they often developed loyal followings within the business managers of one particular nation's 'factory'; the bond was strengthened by the uncertain nature of trade, destabilized both by fluctuating prices in Europe and by irregular production or poor harvests in China. The Co-Hong merchants' monopoly of trade in good times could ensure great prosperity; but they were, at the same time, liable for debts incurred by Western traders allocated to them, and responsible to the Viceroy for the good order of the crews of 'their' Western merchantmen. Bankruptcies among members of the Co-Hong who had bought commodities 'forward' in anticipation of unrealized demand were not uncommon. The real strains in the whole structure developed at the end of the eighteenth century, when Co-Hong members would (or could) no longer stand guarantor for the debts of other members.[14]

Western merchants in Canton normally resided in their own Company building (Pl. 125). We have a good idea of what these 'factories' looked like, lining the waterfront outside the walls of south-western Canton, where the 'foreign factory site' had grown up amongst other Chinese wharf warehouses. In most of the views of the 'Hongs', the buildings occupied by Western Companies stand out for their non-Chinese character; there are elegant arcaded verandahs, baroque porticoes, neo-classical details. But these buildings were not originally custom-built for Western occupants; foreigners were not allowed to own property on the mainland. The flags which always appear flying above the enclosed promenades in front of each building must have been necessary at one time, to identify where a Company had actually founded a trading and residential base that year. The Dutch

Pl. 125. The 'foreign factories' site, or Hong waterfront, at Canton. Chinese School for the expatriate market, c.1835. 58.5 × 44.5 cm.
The Dutch 'factory', identified by its flag, is at the extreme right. The presence of the French flag dates the picture after 1832.

Pl. 126. The deepwater anchorage at Whampoa Reach, c.1850. Chinese School. Overall 81.5 × 46 cm. Taken from hills at the centre of Dane's Island to the south, this shows the well-known panorama of Western merchant ships safely moored twelve miles downriver from the Canton waterfront. The grant of ground for a cemetery, visible in the foreground, was a late concession by the Chinese authorities to the Western trading companies.

records contain constant complaints about the problem of finding suitable space; ships which arrived too late might have to split their Canton-based factors and senior crew among several smaller Hongs, and the Chinese (not surprisingly) extracted the maximum rental from each crew. Only after about mid-century could a Company feel confident that it might occupy the same trading Hong each season, and presumably the rebuilding in Western style dates from these later years.[15]

It is rather surprising that very few such views survive of Batavia, which was far more important to the Dutch than Canton for nearly two centuries, as well as being a provisioning and watering base for crews of most European Companies. Presumably the greatest demand for these 'souvenir' views of Canton, Whampoa Anchorage and Portugal's Macao outpost was when the China trade expanded again after the Napoleonic wars. By then, Batavia had declared itself a revolutionary republic, independent of the VOC, in 1795.

The Canton System evolved to maximize Chinese trading revenues and to minimize disruption to the Chinese social fabric from Western merchants, reflecting the attitude of the Chinese to the sort of trade and commodities which the visitors could bring. The Chinese were remarkably unconcerned whether Westerners came or not. Visitors were (in theory) almost completely banned from entering the walled city of Canton, and resident supercargoes were – until mid-century – forced to return to Macao during the summer months when no ships lay in Whampoa Anchorage. The fact that, despite these restrictions, Westerners still wanted to trade with the Chinese is a reflection of how profitable the return cargoes from Canton really were. The Chinese, to some extent, saw it as an extension of tribute-bearing; they had long tolerated Arab, Korean, Japanese and a variety of South Asian junk-borne traders, because it was implicit that – by trading – these visitors were subjecting themselves to the authority of the 'Middle Kingdom'.

Thus the Chinese perception of overseas trade, preoccupied with Imperial authority, involved very different considerations from the Western one, preoccupied (as the more successfully industrialized countries were) with eliminating the duties and regulations which protected local industry, so as to open up any market which seemed to have potential for absorbing the surplus products of many of the increasingly mechanized Western industries. The Canton System never gave them the opportunity to exploit China in this way, and it required repeated military defeats at Western hands before the Chinese would cede a growing number of new 'treaty ports' which, for the first time, gave Westerners the chance to bypass entirely the bottleneck of the Canton System.

Cargoes from Canton and the Tea Trade

Nothing was more important in a return cargo than the consignment of tea. Tea-trading with China grew significantly in post-1660 Europe, as the fashion for 'soft drinks' – tea, coffee and chocolate – developed at the top of society and the new tastes filtered downwards. As trade revived with post-Civil War China, tea was seen to be a commodity in demand in Europe; porcelain less so, but it had one obvious practical convenience. The expensive wares of the China trade were light-weight and perishable; textiles (primarily finished silks), spices from the mainland, pepper from Java and Sumatra, tea from the uplands in the Chinese coastal provinces, chintzes and other light stuffs from India. Porcelain represented an element within a cargo which could be assembled quickly in Canton; was not wildly subject to vagaries of taste in Europe; did not deteriorate when wet; and enabled an empty ship, moored at Whampoa, to be loaded quickly with a hold flooring of heavy goods, while negotiations took place at Canton for the more important categories of a return cargo.

Thus it was the European demand for tea which came to dominate the whole eighteenth-century overseas trade with China; everything else in a return cargo, although intrinsically valuable, was (in the broadest financial terms) peripheral. Dr Christian Jorg has calculated that, by the middle of the eighteenth century, tea represented on average 70 per cent by value of the total purchases made by a Dutch ship's supercargo in Canton.[16] Silks and spices were profitable; porcelain, though of minor significance in financial terms, has been disproportionately important in the development of Western taste and the customs of civilized society; a few drugs were valuable imports. But tea profitability was the main commercial reason for the existence of the China trade, and great efforts were made to stamp on interlopers in the trade, to gauge the market in Europe, and to pack the prepared leaves, fresh or roasted, for export from Canton and Batavia.

The list of other commodities often brought back from Canton is also interesting, as much for its very limited range as anything. Jorg has summarized the shipping lists. The primary exports were tea, dried and fermented; textiles, including raw and woven silk, and a special high-quality shiny linen from Nanjing which appears in the shipping lists as 'nankeen'; and (in value terms, a poor third) porcelain. Drugs and vegetable products included China root, galingale, anise (strong-smelling, it had to be packed well away from the delicate teas), sago (in which porcelain was often packed),[17] rhubarb and turmeric. There were miscellaneous 'luxury' objects which might on occasion be bought for 'India' shops in the smarter centres of European fashion – painted wallpapers, fans, lacquer, silks, screens. Gold was bought, to trade in India for diamonds but not often to bring back to Europe. And then there were the physically heavy 'ballast' exports, which had, like porcelain, a residual value in the Indian entrepots and Europe: mercury, tin, lead, spelter, sappan wood, rattan, finely grained colonial hardwoods to be cut as exotic veneers and inlays for Western furniture. There were other regular exports. The spice markets of South Asia and India provided unusual flavourings for Western palates, and the Dutch even discovered an excellent market in Canton for pepper from Batavia, showing that the trade in exotic flavourings was not entirely from East to West. Silk was a popular purchase in Canton; the emergent silk industries of the United Kingdom and the Continent repeatedly petitioned for a reduction in the import quotas of finished Chinese silks. Paradoxically, the

Pl. 127. Packing and weighing leaf tea, c.1800. Overall 53.5 × 42.5 cm. From a typical set of twelve gouache paintings on Western rag paper, this is the final view of the tea growing, picking, roasting and wholesaling process. A Western merchant completes negotiations in this massive packing warehouse, while no doubt keeping a watchful eye for any adulteration or short-changing in the consignment he has purchased on the basis of samples tasted earlier.

Chinese finally obliged by banning the export of it in a raw state. Brightly painted Chinese wallpapers with floral patterns on pale pastel grounds, increasingly associated with light and elegant *boiserie*, supplanted the darker wood and the lacquered and painted leather panellings preferred by earlier generations. Fans were imported in tens of thousands and there was a regular market from the early years of the China trade for richly decorated furniture, such as large carved 'Coromandel' screens (in reality, Chinese lacquered ones), nests of lacquered tea tables, and other small, useful furnishings of so-called 'India' origin[18], all of which enhanced a candle-lit formal room.

The tea market was not an easy one to control, for prices in Europe were very variable. Depending on availability and quality, the ships home earliest could make a vastly greater profit from the season's new teas than a laggard. The key to the whole European tea trade was British demand. It is remarkable that the biggest European volume shipping trade in the eighteenth century was smuggling tea from the Continental mainland to Britain, especially along the south coast and East Anglian coastline, where the Dutch, among others, had long traded illegally. The British market was so important that a number of Continental East India Companies, established abroad as monopolies by appropriate royal charter, were in reality little more than fronts for British merchants operating to the Eastern entrepots outside the jurisdiction of the English Company; such was the Ostend Company, and to a lesser extent the Emden and Swedish Companies. British names occur with some regularity as the moving spirits behind these overseas 'front Companies', in particular Colin Campbell, financier behind both the Ostend Company and the Swedish one. It is not surprising that so much space on returning ships was filled with low-value (even if relatively high-profit) porcelain tea table wares.[19]

Western Exports to China

What could Europeans offer the Chinese to finance Canton purchases? This was the perennial problem for all the Companies, because the Chinese considered that they needed or wanted very little from Europe. Over the decades, supercargoes tried an ingenious variety of Western products, each of which they hoped could be developed into a bulk trading commodity. In 1699, the (English) 'New Company' ship *Macclesfield* carried steel sword blades (unlike the Japanese, the Chinese had never been good metal refiners and finishers), domestic glass ware, mirrors, and a large consignment of finished textiles – the English long hoped to turn China and Japan into a market for surplus English cloths.[20] The first ship intended to trade directly to China from the recently independent United States, the *Harriet*, set out in December 1783 with an unlikely cargo of ginseng root, gathered in the woods of New England; a characteristic product of an unindustrialized and undercapitalized country, low on reserves of silver specie after a major war.[21] One Western product always popular in Canton was mechanical toys. Contraptions with moving parts made excellent 'gifts', which passed rapidly up the mandarinate because the demand for amusing articulated mechanical instruments originated from the Palace itself. Clocks, automata, spring-powered scientific instruments; all were very acceptable in Canton, and the clockmaker James Cox had a specific branch of his thriving London business devoted to producing elaborate clocks for the Far Eastern market.

But the market in Canton could only absorb so many swords, roots and automata. In Chapter I, Richard Kilburn has indicated that the thing the Chinese most readily accepted from the West was silver. As the trade, primarily via Canton, recovered in the latter years of the seventeenth century, silver came to represent by far the greatest value in any outgoing cargo from Europe. The real profits in the trade with the Far East lay primarily in what was purchased there, for resale in Europe; the profits did not come from what was taken out to sell. Hence silver was just as useful in entrepots like the Indian ones at Surat and Bengal where, with gold, it was the most saleable commodity with which to buy Indian commodities.

It was to Bengal that another Dutch merchant ship, the *Bredenhof*, set out under the auspices of the Zeeland Chamber in December 1752 with a cargo primarily of silver bullion for the Indian trade. The cargo manifest was listed as fourteen *vaatjes* (barrels) with specially minted VOC copper coins, and thirty chests with silver and gold. This bullion cargo was, in the event, assembled as twenty-nine chests of bar silver, each ingot stamped with the interlocking monogram of the VOC and the initial 'Z' for Zeeland, which represented 300,000 guilders of Heren XVII finance; and one further chest, of five thousand gold ducatoons valued at 25,000 guilders. The silver was specifically intended to be minted into silver rupees at Bengal. The Heren XVII had instructed that specie and copper coins, to a total value of 1,100,000 guilders, should be sent out to Bengal in 1752; an astonishing amount for admittedly a major 'factory'. Carried for safety's sake in three different VOC vessels, the *Bredenhof*'s cargo represented therefore a third of the entire consignment sent out to Bengal to finance the 'factory' trading activities for the year.[22] The ship was wrecked, and we can now see what these silver ingots looked like; not beautiful, but the core financing commodity for the whole China trade.

Pl. 129. Rectangular and shoe-shaped gold ingots from the *Geldermalsen*, c.1750. Rectangular bars 8 cm long, 'Nanking shoes' 5.5 cm wide. Chinese gold bullion was only carried for a few decades in the 18th century on VOC vessels to finance Indian trade, and scarcely any ships are known to have been lost with a cache aboard. The bars are of exceptional historical interest to academic specialists in Far Eastern currency and trade finance, since no other gold bars of this period or type have been published, though wrecks in the future may yield other examples. The cargo contained 145 when the *Geldermalsen* left Canton, but only a total of 125 were recovered from the wreck, as well as a tiny fragment which perhaps made up the weight to a particular value.

Pl. 128. Paste-set, gilt-metal chiming clock in French 'pendule' style for the Chinese market, late 18th century. Made by Chinese craftsmen under Western influence. Ht 54.5 cm.

The Dutch were luckier than many other nations; their base at Batavia had large stocks of silver bullion, tin, lead and iron which could be loaded onto ships heading northwards for the China or Japan trade. Silver coin and bullion long remained the commodity preferred from Europe, until Chinese purchases of Indian opium increased dramatically after the Napoleonic wars. Independent 'country' traders in India and the East, primarily British ones starved of silver from home by the national problem of financing the Continental blockade in Europe, shipped hugely increased quantities of opium to the China coast. For the first time, the opium-buying Chinese were forced to trade back the silver they had been accepting over decades, which was then used to buy the new tea-crop for the huge European market. The process was not direct; Chinese silver, obtained in Canton by illegal trading in opium on non-Company and American ships, was then sold to the English Company factors in Canton, against credits of bills of exchange drawn on the City of London and payable there. So, by this means, 'opium silver' was 'laundered' into the legitimate trade of Canton, and used by the English Company (and many others) to finance its own purchases, since it could not be seen to be itself trading (as an official organization) in the prohibited commodity of opium.[23] The source of the silver had altered, but Westerners had still found only one other commodity which the Chinese would officially trade for in any substantial quantity.

The silver which East Indiamen carried could be obtained from a number of European sources. Traditionally Lisbon, Spanish ports and Antwerp had been the major entrepots for 'New World' bullion flooding into Europe with the annual treasure fleets. The development of Amsterdam as a mercantile centre had been accompanied by its growth as a bullion trading centre, greatly assisted by the flight there of Jewish bullion dealers driven out of Lisbon. (Their splendid Portuguese synagogue still stands near Amsterdam's harbour area.) Amsterdam dealers had also established a lucrative trade buying Spanish colonial pieces-of-eight in Cadiz, for recasting into ingots on the orders of Dutch Chambers. The bars were largely standardized in size, although it was the total weight and purity which mattered, and individual Chambers seem to have cast bars of slightly different shapes and dimensions, no doubt as the exchange rate fluctuated.

THE HISTORY OF THE *GELDERMALSEN*

The *Geldermalsen* was one of six ships commissioned in 1746 by the Zeeland Chamber – after Amsterdam, the second most powerful of the six Chambers of the VOC.[24] The ships were merchant vessels which the VOC used for long-distance trade to the West Indies, and the Far East round the Cape to Batavia, Canton and South Chinese waters. The VOC differed from its great Protestant rival, the English Company, in owning its ships outright. The 'United Company of Merchants of England Trading to the East Indies' chartered ships when it required them at that period, though some ship owners constructed merchantmen only after a charter to the Company had been negotiated in advance. The *Geldermalsen* was larger than most comparable English ships, though the tonnage of English ships was often understated in the official records; ships with a declared capacity of more than 500 tons had a statutory obligation to carry a chaplain! Even so, at her declared metric weight of 1,155 tons, the *Geldermalsen* was substantial; some 150 feet long and 42 feet wide, her construction took ten months, and she was eventually handed over to the Chamber in July 1747.[25] The larger of the ship's bells which Hatcher recovered records the safe delivery of this new addition to the fleet of the Zeeland Chamber. She was named after the country estate of the Zeeland director, Jan Van Borssele.[26]

Her first trip to the East was a prolonged and leisurely affair, typical of the random journeys that these trading ships so often undertook. Cargoes could be traded a dozen times, even under the baleful eye of the Heren XVII in Holland or the Hoge Regering at Batavia. The *Geldermalsen* left Holland in August 1748, and arrived in Batavia next March. Despatched thence to Japan, a seven-month return trip saw her back in Batavia with a cargo from the Dutch 'factory' at Deshima, the only Western Company post still permitted by the Japanese to trade on their mainland. A trip to Canton, loading goods for the important Dutch 'factory' at Surat in north-west India, occupied over a year until the laden ship docked in Gujurat in March 1751. But it was then rechartered, to return to Canton; and there, in July 1751, it joined a group of three other Dutch merchant vessels load-ing cargoes of Chinese goods to take directly home to the Netherlands. The ship was not in good condition, and it required an extensive overhaul in Whampoa Reach until the new captain, Jan Diederik Morel, was satisfied that she was suffi-ciently seaworthy to begin the arduous trip home as soon as prevailing north-easterly monsoon winds would permit.

The fare on board did not promise to be exciting. Morel found that provisions were low and he had to stock up from the other Dutch ships, because the Batavia base, apparently contrary to custom, had sent nothing for the trip. The waterbutts were mouldy; Morel asked Batavia for twenty fresh casks to be shipped for the *Geldermalsen*, which he could take aboard in the Sunda Straits at the same time, as the plan was, that the secret consignment of gold intended for Batavia could be taken off without stopping there. At this stage of the continuous tension between the Heren XVII and the Hoge Regering as to whether ships should invariably stop at Batavia, or bypass it on both outward and homeward journeys to China, a compromise had been reached whereby ships traded at Batavia on the outward journey, but went home without pausing there to reprovision or collect mer-chandise; their 'China' ships thus returned with the tea as fresh as possible.

There were some surprising inclusions in the *Geldermalsen*'s passenger and crew list. An English merchant, Richard Bagge, had paid for a berth in the Great Cabin, to ensure him a quicker arrival at Batavia than an English ship from Whampoa could provide at that time. Meanwhile the ship's crew was strengthened by sixteen English seamen, part of a group of thirty-six poached in Canton by VOC officials, contrary to the regular agreement not to deplete the crews of rival ships. This extra group brought the ship's complement probably to 112; of this crew, only thirty-two would survive the disaster a fortnight after leaving on 18 December, 1751. The captain, first and second mate were all lost, as were many of the thirty or more soldiers who formed a surprisingly large element in the crew. There is no record of how many of the British contingent of seamen survived; nor of the fate of the unexpected solitary North American colonial, a New Yorker called Lourens Bolden. Why did this routine voyage end in disaster?

As far as one can judge, it was entirely a result of navigational error. The weather was good, and the wind, as anticipated, blew from the north for this section of straightforward route, heading south from the Macao Roads. The ship had been sailing for sixteen days, and, although maps and navigational charts of the period were inexact, the Dutch had had enormous experience in these waters. The familiar landmarks were checked off, and soundings were regularly taken to confirm safe depths, especially if the charts showed any indication of shoaling. Certainly the captain showed no sign of unease that afternoon. A long and perhaps generously wined dinner kept him in his cabin till 3.30 in the afternoon; he then came on deck to check the ship's location with the third watch, Christoffel van Dijk, the most senior crew member to survive the wrecking. Van Dijk gave the crucial information to Morel that the island landmark they were awaiting

Pl. 132 (right). Chinese rectangular gold ingot, one of 107, from the *Geldermalsen* cargo, c.1750. 8 cm long, 2.5 cm deep, 1.5 cm high at the slightly raised edge.
The double-gourd reserve at the centre is impressed with the characters 'yuan ji', and the square-seal characters each read 'bao'. The phrase 'yuan ji bao', found on many of the rectangular bars only, translates as 'treasure' or 'gold ingot'. It is most unlikely that these bars were minted with the Western export market in mind. Nevertheless, the *Geldermalsen* archives record that the Co-Hong bullion supplier in Canton had difficulty completing this Dutch order from his source in Nanjing ('Nanking') because of earlier VOC purchases for Surat, and rival demand also from English and French Company supercargoes who were forced to pay substantially higher prices for their deliveries.

Pl. 131 (below). Base of soapstone seal, monogrammed 'F.B.', probably for Frederick Berkenhouwer, a native of Brandenburg recorded as 'senior master' on the *Geldermalsen*'s crew list of 1751. *Heirloom and Howard.*

during this stretch of South China Sea, Het Ruyge Eiland, lay behind them already, visible to the north-west. The captain knew this meant that one of the more dangerous reefs on this part of the route, Geldria's Droogte, had been successfully avoided. It featured on the VOC charts of the period, and would have certainly entailed a court martial for any captain whose ship strayed onto it from the correct shipping lane. The ship's course was altered to take account of the apparent position.[27]

Three hours later, just past sunset, the boatswain (one Urbanus Urbani) was occupied with the anchors, affording him from the deck a view ahead of the ship. Even in the near-darkness, he saw breakers, always a sign of a reef very near the surface. The ship must have been extremely close; he yelled for the steersman to swing the ship off its southerly course, but it was too late and the ship hit the reef. As Captain Hatcher found, the bulk of the coral reef is now some six or nine metres below the surface, but the ship hit it very heavily. Preserving his calm with the benefit of his VOC naval experience, the captain gave orders for an emergency resetting of the sails. The ship tore free of the reef in an easterly direction. At this point Morel's professionalism for some reason cracked. There must have been considerable uncertainty among the motley crew, and in the chaos Morel gave a new instruction for setting the sails which unavoidably slewed the ship back onto a southerly tack. Slamming into the reef a second time, the ship suffered major damage. The records suggest that it was this second violent impact which caused the ship to be lost. The forepart was badly damaged, and gravel ballast began to spill out onto the coral reef, as Hatcher was to discover two centuries later. That porcelain which is known from the packing invoices to have been on board, but is now missing from the quantity recovered, may well have been near the bow and hence damaged at this moment of second impact.

As far as one can tell from the records, there was no panic. Miscellaneous articles were lowered down and the lifeboats (launched more or less successfully) began to fill with the first of the crew to abandon the listing, leaking ship, taking with them two drawers from a desk full of currency – and the quartermaster had maps with him.

The gold was not an immediate priority at this stage of the escape. Maybe the captain hoped that the ship could survive, and there would be no need to bring this heavy and confidential box from its hiding place in the cabin below decks. He only sent for it at the last moment. One of the survivors recorded that he and another crew member were ordered to bring an unidentified but weighty chest up to the deck. Before they could lower it overboard, the ship began to list more heavily. The heavy chest must have lain right on deck at one side until just before the capsizing ship sank down to the seabed, because Hatcher found the ingots of gold just outside the hull. They were partially concealed under a mound of decayed brickwork, all that remained of the brick-lined galley deep in the ship. Eighty men were lost with the ship; it was a tale of navigational error, incorrect procedure in an emergency, and – on the evidence of the archives – slow reaction by Captain Morel when the ship was clearly not going to survive, and the consignment of gold might have been saved from the stricken hulk.

This was certainly the view of the very critical authorities at Batavia when the two boatloads of survivors reached it a week later, and made their report to the Hoge Regering. The considered judgement was that the two lifeboats had left the site too quickly; it was inexcusable to lose three-quarters of the crew, and had the gold really disappeared? There had been time to launch the boats, bring out drawerfuls of States currency ('rixdollars'), a compass, barrels of biscuits and water, and even pick up a piglet that was found floundering as the last survivor of the fresh cargo of twenty pigs. The suspicion was compounded by the fact that the most senior surviving crew member was the boatswain and third mate, Christoffel van Dijk; the very same man whose initial report to the captain had prompted the fatal change of course. The Hoge Regering reduced him to the ranks of an ordinary seaman as punishment for his orders to leave the reef area too early before a final effort had been made in the darkness to locate survivors. Later that year he was sent back to face further examination in the Netherlands. Happily, he was reinstated in Holland by the Heren XVII and he reappears later in the VOC roll as a 'third master'. In the light of Hatcher's discovery of the cache, van Dijk's story about the gold seems to have been true. All the same, Hatcher did fail to locate twenty-two of the 147 bars supposed to be on board, when he and his divers scoured the small and specific area where the bulk of this splendid treasure was found.[28]

The extensive shipping records give much information about the background to the gold and porcelain which survived. Jorg and his archivists worked intensively before the auction on a fascinating comparison, trying to match the detailed 'Requirements for the 1751 Return Cargoes', sent out from the Netherlands indirectly to Canton, with the actual pots discovered. But, as they worked, it became increasingly apparent that there were major inconsistencies between what should have been on board, and what was actually loaded on board in 1751, as noted in packing lists at the time. The Requirements for 1751 instructed, for example, that certain specific shapes should not be bought that year; the sick pots in the shape of children's chamber pots were not wanted in Europe that season. Yet the packing lists showed that 606 were actually shipped, and Hatcher recovered 495 of them. This apparent insouciance to VOC instructions can be matched in a number of other categories. The invoices mention that 100 more dinner services were purchased in Canton than the Heren XVII actually wanted. For the *Geldermalsen*, the

packing records are a little patchy, but the solitary remaining letter to the Zeeland Chamber, owner of the vessel, has been analysed by Jorg in relation to the Requirements. This suggests what seems to have happened at Canton, and why the present 'Nanking Cargo' differs so much from the 223,303 pieces of porcelain and fifty dinner services actually requested.[29]

The problem was that the written Requirements for 1751 did not get through to Canton in time.[30] Specific types of object, for which drawings and models were sent out that year, were not purchased; conversely, specific prohibitions for that year were ignored. The supercargoes' concern to load a flooring of porcelain as quickly as possible after the ship received maintenance at Whampoa meant that they could not afford to wait in the expectation of the orders arriving via Batavia. There was a companion ship in Canton, the *Amstelveen*, on which the remainder of the actual purchases made in 1751 were loaded; but these amounted to only some twenty crates.[31] The bulk of that year's porcelain purchases, some 203 crates, were on the *Geldermalsen*. The contents recovered by Hatcher, as well as the documentary evidence, led Jorg to an inescapable conclusion: that the supercargoes in 1751 relied, in the absence of new ones, on the orders for 1750 as their basis for buying porcelain. It was not unusual for there to be a year's time lag before purchases left Canton on the next available ship. Indeed, with the exception of the twenty crates mentioned above, the *Amstelveen*'s entire cargo comprised porcelain bought by supercargoes the year before, during the 1750 trading season, but not shipped the previous year. By the same token, the packing records for 1752, the year after the loss of the *Geldermalsen*, indicate that the *Luxemburg* would have been carrying 172 crates of porcelain, much of that purchases made the year before by supercargoes from the *Geldermalsen* and *Amstelveen*, but not shipped home with them. The cargo shipped in December 1751, the one which Hatcher's crew found, was therefore not at all what Jorg's researchers anticipated from the original orders that year supplied by the Heren XVII. There is no evidence that the porcelain-purchasing instructions for 1751 were ever acted on by the supercargoes in Canton. Whatever was in stock there that autumn was added to the goods purchased in 1750, but not shipped the year before. That part of the new purchases which could not be accomodated on board the two ships in the autumn of 1751 was held over until the next year. As the *Luxemburg*'s 1752 packing lists show, these remaining purchases from 1751 were then shipped uneventfully to the Netherlands, along with the newer porcelains correctly purchased as the Requirements for 1752 requested. The Requirements for purchasing porcelain in Canton in the latter years of the 1740s barely changed from year to year; it was sad that the effort by the Heren XVII, in 1751, to initiate new lines and import novel categories of Chinese export porcelain should have been so fruitless![32]

Jorg and his researchers unearthed much fascinating information during their investigations into the cargo, but none perhaps is so valuable as their detective work into its unexpected composition. The archive evidence confirms the impression that, with the exception of a few 'private trade' wares (which would vary from year to year depending on what an individual wanted) the *Geldermalsen*'s porcelain cargo should be seen as a typical shipment made by any of the active East India Companies returning from the Far East. The cargo should be understood in an international mid-eighteenth century China trade context, which the documentary research has revealed in extraordinary detail for us, and for which the porcelain provides dramatic and tangible evidence.

Pl. 133. Chinese shoe-shaped gold ingot, one of only eighteen, from the *Geldermalsen* cargo, c.1750. Basically an oval bar with raised ends and a rounded underside, the 'Nanking shoe' has entered Chinese mythology as an emblem of wealth carried by Immortals or deities. The shape is believed to derive from the early version of a lady's shoe, shaped to accommodate the 'bound foot' characteristic of a distinguished or courtly female. It is know to coin specialists as 'sycee' bullion, and a comparable shape can also be found minted in silver. But, until 1890, gold never formed the basis of a ciruclating currency minted in small denominations; copper coinage, threaded on long strings ('strings of cash'), long remained the basis of smaller transactions.

Many of the *Geldermalsen*'s 'shoe' ingots are stamped within the 'pinched' recesses at the sides with the Chinese character '*ji*', meaning 'happiness'; stamped twice, as most are, the reading should thus be the thoroughly auspicious wish, for the owner or recipient of one of these classic Chinese emblems of wealth, of 'double happiness'. It is also very likely that the impressed seals found on both kinds of gold bar were required as proof of the carat content.

THE CARGO OF CERAMICS

The recovered ceramics consist almost entirely of blue and white wares, wares with 'Chinese Imari' decoration (underglaze blue, overglaze iron-red enamel and gold), and the remainder with overglaze enamel decoration in now unidentifiable colours, mostly degraded to blackish. Despite being packed very tightly in what appears from contemporary packing lists usually to have been sago, rice husks or paper, the overglaze enamels have softened and in very many cases disappeared. The wares which were originally simply 'blue and white', with no enamel decoration over the glaze, have thus survived best the effect of saltwater immersion; the glaze is mostly in excellent condition.

The *Geldermalsen* has yielded porcelain with a number of unusual designs. But it is 'East India Company' ware, purchased on a conservative basis for a market which was regular in its demands. Not for the supercargoes the speculative excitement of 'private trade' purchases on behalf of their Company; the bottom of the *Geldermalsen*'s hull contained the types of porcelain that sold, year after year, in massive uneventful auctions, where by the 1750s prices had stabilized, and in some years even fallen, since the headier days of the Kangxi period. Blue and white plates, sold wholesale in England in the early 1700s for 15 pence, were retailing fifty years later for only 10 pence,[33] but still the Companies poured this routine enamelled or blue and white porcelain into Europe. It was 'useful' porcelain, for the most part blue and white; domestic crockery of a type popular all over Europe in genteel households which did not aspire to glamorously enamelled armorial wares. In 1749–50 enamelled wares represented less than one tenth of these 'useful' wares brought back to England by the English Company.[34]

The cargo reveals exactly those qualities in Chinese export porcelain which Western buyers had come to appreciate and expect, and which Western potters sought constantly to reproduce and emulate. Brightness, translucence, thinness, resonance, strength and cheapness; these were all qualities which contemporary

Pl. 134. Blue and white Peony and Pomegranate pattern plates, c.1750. 23 cm diam.

English and French soft-paste manufacturers were unsuccessful in matching for technical reasons, and which German hard-paste manufacturers could only match at colossal expense and with royal subsidies. But, within a very few decades of the ill-fated homeward voyage of the *Geldermalsen*, the situation in European ceramics had changed dramatically. The death knell for these massive sales of Chinese export in Europe was sounded by two technical innovations, whose commercial possibilities were most successfully exploited in England in the 1760s and 1770s. One was the introduction of a new kind of thin and resilient pottery called 'Queen's Ware', or creamware (Pl. 135). It was turned into a commercial winner by the astute businessman-potter Josiah Wedgwood, who built up an enormous creamware export business to Continental Europe and Colonial America.[35] The other was the successful innovation of printing engravings (taken from copper plate patterns specially commissioned to fit a certain shape of vessel) onto, or under, the glaze on all kinds of low-fired pottery and higher-fired porcelains by 'transferring' the image (inked on a sheet of thin material) onto the ceramic surface. This made it far cheaper to reproduce elaborate patterns in Western taste; enabled potters to respond quickly to changing demand and taste in designs; and helped to achieve a very consistent quality of decoration. From about 1620, it was Chinese porcelain which had entirely dominated the commercial market in Europe for fine ceramics, filling the gap between the cheapest wood or ceramic crocks, and metal table vessels (ranging from pewter to gold). Over the last few decades of the eighteenth century, this stranglehold was totally eliminated. After 1784, only in the eastern seaboard of newly emancipated North America could Chinese 'standard' wares still compete, as American traders began to bring them back from Canton directly to Salem, New York, Rhode Island, Baltimore and Philadelphia. 'Nanking'-type blue and white wares had fallen victim to the scientific revolution in the British potteries. The *Geldermalsen* cargo comes at the end of the era of oriental ceramics dominating Western schemes of interior decoration; it captures a moment of European taste in transition under the impulse of the new technologies born of the Industrial Revolution.

Thus, for anyone interested in the history of early modern European taste, the *Geldermalsen* cargo helps to explain why the idea of decorative blue and white porcelain was for so long associated in the Western mind with a Chinese origin. And for the technically minded, it well illustrates the confident ability of mid-eighteenth century Chinese potters to produce, in vast quantities and to a consistently high standard, fine porcelain of a type unmatched in price and quality anywhere in Europe.

The ceramics were recovered by Hatcher from the remaining section of the hull under three feet of silt and tea.[36] They form an undisturbed, homogeneous group of wares destined quite specifically for the Western market, a ship heading home with a commercial cargo that, over the decades, could be expected to sell easily, regularly and profitably in Europe. Since the main consideration was to fit as much porcelain as possible into a limited space, the simpler-shaped pieces (packed tightly in sets or stacks) were chosen by the VOC supercargoes for the essentially conservative buying preferences of the Heren XVII.

There are several obvious divisions within the physical composition of the cargo. Among the Company purchases, the tea wares represent two-thirds of the porcelain recovered, but carry an astonishingly narrow range of designs; the table-wares form a striking group; and the other 'shaped' vessels on board reflect mid-century, specifically European demand. Finally, there is a small but interesting group, part of the profitable 'private trade' allowance which entitled senior members of the crew to fill a certain amount of hull space with purchases on their own account, to trade at an appropriate stage or retain as mementoes.

By this date the vast proportion of ceramic wares made for both native and overseas markets is believed to have come from Jingdezhen, south Jiangxi Province. This accepted belief is difficult either to verify or to contradict, given the absence of export wares excavated on the mainland, the extreme rarity of observant contemporary visitors to China getting any distance inland past the coastal ports, and the monopolist position of Canton as the hub of overseas trade for Westerners. The extensive Ming ceramics export trade involved more provincially manufactured categories, such as the heavy celadon-glazed dishes and bowls of Zhejiang Province. Not so, by 1751; Canton was the port at which to trade, and the ceramics seem to have come almost entirely from Jingdezhen. Ships might still venture north to Amoy or Ningbe but there was no guarantee that, even if they found a port with pots (or anything more desirable) for sale, the local bureaucracy would allow them to trade, in view of the Imperial edicts about the Pearl River entrepot.

Jingdezhen lay several hundred miles inland and the transport of finished and undecorated glazed ceramics to Canton complicated arrangements for Co-Hong merchants providing current stock. The trading season at Canton was too short for local Chinese merchants to commission porcelain in novel shapes or with new designs from Jingdezhen for delivery the same season to the Canton entrepot. The custom therefore developed in Canton of leaving designs to be made up, for delivery during the next season. This appears regularly in the Canton archives only from mid-century, Co-Hong merchants holding substantial stocks in direct anticipation of Western demand when ships arrived. This change may well have been associated with an administrative change in Canton. Hitherto ship captains and visitors to the Hongs had to leave their comfortable but all-bachelor residences at the end of each season, to return to what the English diarist William Hickey depicted contemptuously as the decrepit, run-down Portuguese colony at Macao on the south-easterly exit of the Pearl River, where at least they returned to the company of ladies. Having a resident Council continuously staffing each Hong obviously helped regularize the ordering and supplying of porcelain, though it could never become non-seasonal as long as ships were sail-driven, and the trading season was determined by the constraints of monsoon winds, their direction shifting dramatically from south-easterly in summer to north-easterly in winter. Special commission wares such as armorial services and individual wares for the British market seem to have reached a peak at this period, to judge from surviving examples.[37] The custom evolved of local enamellers in Canton, furnished with watercolour or print designs by visiting Westerners, copying them in overglaze enamels onto entirely white-glazed wares, or (in rarer cases) completing in overglaze enamels a design partially executed at Jingdezhen in underglaze blue. Having special commissions enamelled locally, fired in low-temperature muffle kilns, greatly speeded production and made control easier. Unfortunately very few 'private trade' or 'special commission' wares seem to have survived the wreck. The crates containing the purchases by individuals were more vulnerable, normally stacked higher up the hold than the Company cargo and loaded later during the ship's sojourn at Whampoa into any interstices left when the Company cargo had been firmly secured.

'Private trade' could take many forms, although porcelain must have been a favoured (and profitable) commodity on homeward journeys, to judge from the quantity which survived. William Hickey, travelling from China in 1770 on the English Company ship the *Plassey*, recorded that a bad storm seriously damaged the masts but the captain was able to buy replacements from the 'private cargo' carried on board by the carpenter. During the return journey from Canton, Hickey had a very narrow escape during a storm; the captain's 'private trade',

Pl. 136. A porcelain shop, Chinese School, c.1830.
A retail merchant with an unexceptional stock of standard wares and shapes waits for a Western supercargo to examine his samples; this scene is normally the last in an album depicting porcelain production. *Private collection.*

which consisted of huge baulks of oriental rosewood, became detached from the battens securing it in the Great Cabin and came within an ace of fracturing the diarist's skull as he tossed fitfully in his hammock. Canton offered many exotic and profitable trifles and commodities, to sell when a ship berthed in Europe.

Pl. 137. Stacks of blue and white Pagoda Riverscape pattern bowls and saucers, large size, c.1750. Bowls 7.5 cm diam, saucers 12 cm diam.

The Tea-Table Wares

The latter part of the seventeenth century was characterized by the rise of the 'soft drinks' industry, as tea, coffee and chocolate became available in unprecedented quantities; non-alcoholic alternative drinks for all social occasions.[38] The porcelain trade from China was crucially influenced by this development. The *Geldermalsen* was carrying a very substantial cargo of handleless small bowls and saucers; a smaller group of tea pots; and a few handled cups, which have been identified as being specifically intended for serving chocolate. There was clearly a considerable percentage profit in importing handleless coffee, chocolate and tea bowls and saucers; of all the wares available to buy, they could be packed with the greatest compactness. Their survival rate on the *Geldermalsen* was remarkably high, despite the shuddering crashes as it smashed twice into the virtually submerged reef. The quantities imported throughout the century, by every East India Company bringing porcelain home, reflect the enormous retail demand for sets of Chinese tea-table wares. The VOC archives suggest a very steady 200 per cent gross profit on tea bowls and saucers at mid-century.[39] International wholesalers could risk buying the vast lots, unloaded through annual East India Company auctions throughout Europe each year. Society at all levels required coffee, tea and chocolate sets, tea pots and other ceramic accoutrements for their civilized entertaining.

'Conversation' pieces, portraits of families gathered informally, frequently show the way in which these tea wares were actually assembled and handled. The informative family tea party suggests the way in which a tea table would be laid, perhaps a decade before the *Geldermalsen*'s departure from Canton. The tea is in a sealed caddy, and spoons in a 'spoon tray'; a pair of sugar cutters or tongs lies near a bowl with the cover off, and a saucer-dish probably contains some kind of sweet wafer. The tea kettle is kept hot on an elegant stand with an oil burner beneath it, and another tall jug would have contained milk, or perhaps coffee, frequently served at the same time (Pl. 138). Tea was clearly drunk from the cup itself, held in this case in the right hand, not from the saucer; a 'dish of tea' was no longer the fashionable way to take the beverage, though this varied between class and country. (As late as 1880, the Danish painter Exter depicted a 'genre' tea party with tea being drunk from the saucer.) A slop-bowl was an indispensable part of the service, the tea made by infusing a few leaves in individual cups, to be replaced with another pinch of leaves when the infusion had lost its savour. The porcelain teapot could not have been kept warm over a burner in the same way as the silver one was, so this probably led to a more regular requirement for hot-water jugs, to refill the cooling and emptied pot. The *Geldermalsen*'s cargo, unfortunately, casts little light on these changes, although recovered 'private cargo' includes a few tea-drinking accessories not apparently available in the Company's purchases, presumably from individual services bought for personal use.

Jorg's researches enable us to differentiate between the three main types of 'hot beverage' serving cups.[40] Hitherto the shipping inventories and, even more so, the rare auction sale catalogues have been very imprecise about the function of different kinds of cup and bowl. Often the handleless bowls are referred to in contemporary documents as 'cups', further complicating the issue. We always think of a cup as having a handle, after tea services began to have both handled 'cups' for coffee and handleless 'bowls' for tea. We can now with rather more confidence

identify between tea, coffee and chocolate cups, because Jorg has discovered a
number of original drawings which accompanied the VOC annual statements of
'Requirements for the Return Cargoes'.[41] It is still unclear whether these variously
shaped bowls were used in different ways and combinations, depending on the
nationality and social status of the owner.

The *Geldermalsen* does not appear to have contained, as Company cargo, any tea
sets with all the accessories matching. Jorg has noted that, although many
complete sets had been shipped before 1745, none were bought in the period
1745–50. The *Geldermalsen* suggests that this was true of 1751 as well,[42] and that
the ship was carrying massive but random purchases of bowls and saucers, not
assembled complete sets.

The composition of tea services expanded throughout the eighteenth century,
according to the VOC archives. In 1729 they indicate that a full tea set should
consist of a tea pot and stand, milk jug and stand, slop bowl, sugar bowl with lid
and stand (the latter is rarely found in surviving services), twelve tea bowls and
saucers, six chocolate cups with handles and six without. Coffee was a beverage to
be drunk more in a coffee house rather than at home; whereas social tea drinking
at home was very much a female occupation at this date in the Netherlands. Jorg
has found the first mention of composite tea and coffee services in 1758, but there
is no record that the VOC ever bought coffee services on their own. These larger
sets comprised a coffee pot and stand, tea pot and stand, milk jug and stand, tea
caddy, slop bowl and under-dish, covered sugar bowl with stand, twelve coffee
cups and saucers, twelve tea cups and saucers, and six chocolate cups. Separate
porcelain chocolate pots are never itemized, except for one instance in 1776;
probably they were less successful in porcelain than tea and coffee pots, since the
cooling chocolate would thicken and the pot could hardly be kept hot over a spirit
lamp.

The *Geldermalsen*'s massive and apparently random cargo of handleless bowls confirms that it was 'Chinamen' who assembled complete retail sets in the Netherlands from bulk purchases. Not until 1791 were supercargoes asked to buy large amounts of matching elements for complete services which could be assembled in the Netherlands for auctioning; until then, sets for the Dutch market were apparently purchased only as 'private cargo'.

The variously sized bowls and saucers appear in the archives with specific names, differentiated by shape and size. All, except chocolate cups, had diameters greater than their height. Cups with handles were normally almost twice as expensive as those without, and equally sold for more in Holland.

The tea cups formed standard identifiable groups; large (Groot), double (Dubbel), single Dutch (Enkel Hollands), small Dutch (Klein Hollands), and doll tea service (Poppegoed). This easy distinction was confused by the fact that the large-size tea bowl was similar to the single-size coffee cups and saucers. The VOC

Pl. 140. Blue and white Blue Pine pattern bowl and saucer,
large size, c.1750. Bowl 7.5 cm diam, saucer 11 cm diam.

Pl. 141. Blue and white Pagoda Riverscape pattern bowl and saucer,
large size, c.1750. Bowl 7.5 cm diam, saucer 12 cm diam.

Pl. 142. Blue and enamelled Imari
Pavilion pattern bowl and saucer,
c.1750. Bowl 7.5 cm diam, saucer
11.5 cm diam.

Requirements indicate that the height of a standard tea bowl or cup was normally
5–6 centimetres, and the diameter slightly larger, at 6–7 centimetres. Deep saucers
were regarded as old-fashioned in Holland, though this preference may have
varied elsewhere in Europe. Prices seem to have varied remarkably little over the
century; a single-size blue and white tea cup cost 7 cents in 1731, 8 cents in 1760,
and 7 cents in 1785. For the same years, an enamelled one cost 12, 12 and 10 cents,
and an 'Imari' one was 14, 10 and 15 cents.[44]

The coffee cups were purchased in three basic sizes; double coffee cups and
saucers (Dubbel Koffiegoed), large Dutch size (Groot Hollands Koffiegoed), and
standard single Dutch size (Enkel Hollands Koffiegoed). As with tea cups, the
handleless variety were shipped in vastly greater quantities than ones with awk-
ward handles, and cost less to purchase in Canton. Single ones measured 6.5 centimetres high, and 7.5 centimetres diameter; the larger sizes were probably up to 9.5
centimetres diameter, and regularly cost about 50 per cent more than the single
ones. The archives show that blue and white single-size coffee cups, which were
for practical purposes identical to the large tea cups, cost 9 cents in 1732;
enamelled ones cost 13 cents. In 1760 the respective prices were 8 and 12 cents; by
1785 they stood at 10 and 12 cents. For all palettes, double coffee cups cost about
50 per cent more than single during the period; one wonders what occasion
required larger servings of coffee and tea, to justify buying substantially more
expensive cups.[45]

The cargo of chocolate cups on the *Geldermalsen* was relatively very small. It was acceptable to drink chocolate from cups both with and without handles until about the mid-1750s, but after then Jorg suggests it was more normal to use cups with handles, although both kinds were still being shipped in 1760 and their purchase price was surprisingly the same: 14 cents for blue and white ones. The main distinguishing characteristic of a chocolate cup was its dimensions; according to the VOC Requirements in 1761, the diameter and height should both be 7 centimetres, and the diameter was never greater than the height. Chocolate services never seem to have existed on their own – the cups were always part of larger tea, or tea and coffee, services. The VOC only once shipped a service with a chocolate pot, which may or may not have had the necesssary hole in the cover for stirring this thicker beverage with a long spoon. Western collectors sometimes think of chocolate cups as having two handles on the sides of the body, not one, but the drawings which accompanied the VOC Requirements in 1758 illustrate none with two handles under designs for chocolate cups. The *Geldermalsen* had chocolate cups with two sorts of handles, both owing something to European originals. One handle with loop scallops appears to derive from an early form found on Meissen tea wares, and the cups are decorated in Chrysanthemum Rock pattern in the standard three palettes; the simpler version has a plain loop handle, on a tall cup decorated with flowers only in badly degraded enamels.[46]

For tea-drinking, as opposed to coffee or chocolate, Jorg's evidence complements that compiled by Helen Detweiler from American retailers' advertisements several decades later. This suggests that, in America at least, some eighteenth-century drinkers of tea distinguished quite precisely between the two available sizes of tea bowl. The larger was understood to be for breakfast sets, the smaller for the mid-afternoon or early evening 'tea party'. Detweiler has examined the way in which even the sober George Washington followed changing fashions in American polite society for table and tea ceramics, by ordering for Mount Vernon and elsewhere, at regular intervals, new types of services or pieces with new forms of decoration: the proviso being, as he wrote in 1758, 'pray let them be neat and

Pl. 143. Blue and enamelled Bamboo and Pine pattern bowl and saucer, c.1750. Bowl 7.5 cm diam, saucer 11.5 cm diam.

Pl. 144. Enamelled Daisy Fence
pattern chocolate cup, c.1750. Cup
6.5 cm diam, saucer 13 cm diam.

Pl. 145. Blue and white
Chrysanthemum Rock pattern
chocolate cup and saucer, c.1750.
Cup 7 cm diam, saucer 13 cm diam.

Pl. 146. Blue and enamelled Chrysanthemum Rock pattern chocolate cup and saucer, c.1750.
Cup 7 cm diam, saucer 13 cm diam.

Pl. 147. Enamelled Chrysanthemum Rock pattern chocolate cup and saucer, c.1750.
Cup 6.5 cm diam, saucer 13 cm diam.

Pl. 148. Jan Josef Horemans the Elder (1682-1759). A Dutch bourgeois interior with ladies taking tea. 47.6 × 57.8 cm.

fashionable or send none.'[47] Chinese porcelain, not imports from Europe, remained the sort preferred by Tidewater Virginia tobacco planters for entertaining at dinner and tea, which is where Washington sheds light on the *Geldermalsen*'s cargo.[48] In the orders sent to the London 'Chinaman', Robert Farrer and Company, Washington differentiated by function regularly between breakfast cups (a dozen such, 'for breakfasting', were ordered in September 1765), and smaller ones for afternoon tea.[49] What is not clear is how, or if, these cups were differentiated in commercial rather than domestic use. From 1758 onwards, Jorg has identified VOC orders differentiating between coffee and tea services. But the big commercial establishments requiring huge quantities of such drinking cups, the 'coffee houses', had by then long established themselves, especially in London, as the fashionable daily meeting places to read papers, catch up on the gossip, dine and discuss politics. How or when did they use four or five different sizes of cup and bowl for serving different beverages? In the cargo of small bowls and matching saucers, there are two examples where the same design appears on bowls in two differing sizes: the Blue Pine pattern and the Pagoda Riverscape pattern, both available in tens of thousands of pieces. Was this so that an all-purpose tea and coffee service could be assembled in the same design, for morning and afternoon requirements; or did the coffee houses use the larger handleless bowls for coffee and the smaller, as the Mount Vernon records suggest, only for 'after-dinner' tea?

The matter is further complicated by a surprising absence of handled coffee cups on the *Geldermalsen*. The style was widely used in tea and coffee services of the period, but the only handled cups are identified unequivocally (by the drawings) as chocolate cups (Pls. 144–7). And yet there are many examples extant of

Pl. 149. Jan Josef Horemans the Elder (1682-1759). *Tea party in a Netherlandish garden: Springtime.* 48.5 × 40.4 cm. Note the brown tea bowls and saucers, the blue slop bowl, and the metal tea pot. The brown wares appear to match very closely the 'Batavian' wares; given the apparently short time when this brown-glazed porcelain was popular, it is interesting that Horemans should have used these tea wares as studio props.

armorial handled cups, the cup greater in height than diameter, which are always called coffee cups to distinguish them from tea bowls. They were significantly more expensive to buy and ship (because of the inconvenient and fragile handle). Did coffee houses stick for general usage to the heavily potted, somewhat coarser and large handleless bowls, like the so-called 'Batavian' ones with brown-glazed exteriors, which were recovered in such quantities from the *Geldermalsen*?[50] Jorg points out that the VOC Requirements specify some bowls are to be handleless and of 'very thick porcelain', which would make them rather expensive coarse wares, as export dues from Canton were assessed on the weight of the crates. The records indicate that coffee-house ware was first shipped in 1752, and the last shipment of this somewhat unsuccessful line happened in 1758. The *Geldermalsen* evidence suggests that as early as 1751, specific coffee-house wares were being made and exported by the VOC. The wastage rate must have been far greater for the vessels used in commercial establishments. This may perhaps explain why coarse quality ones (like the 'Batavian' ones) are less common nowadays in Europe than finer quality ones, which often have a coat-of-arms or personal device suggesting that they were always more expensive 'special commission' purchases, and have survived more genteel handling.

Pl. 150. Brown-glazed blue and white Batavian Willow pattern coffee cup and saucer, c.1750.
Cup 8.5 cm diam, saucer 13 cm diam.

Pl. 151. Brown-glazed blue and white Batavian Bamboo and Peony pattern coffee cup and saucer,
c.1750. Cup 7.5 cm diam, saucer 11.5 cm diam.

Pl. 152. Brown-glazed blue and white Batavian Bamboo and Chrysanthemum pattern coffee cup
and saucer, c.1750. Cup 8.5 cm diam, saucer 13 cm diam.

Pl. 153. Brown-glazed blue and white Batavian Pavilion pattern coffee cup and saucer, c.1750.
Cup 8.5 cm diam, saucer 13.5 cm diam.

The Designs on the Tablewares

The designs on the *Geldermalsen* flatwares (plates and dishes) and tablewares are surprisingly limited in range and only rarely particularly outstanding in terms of Chinese decoration. By and large, they are carefully tailored to fill the available space contained within the well and the wide-flanged border. The designs formed part of the standard canon of Jingdezhen ornament on export-quality commercial ceramics; designs which were a crucial source of inspiration to Western potters, looking for subjects to paint on their products in exotic foreign taste. The *Geldermalsen* is an invaluable sealed time capsule for any historian establishing a chronology for these changing but standard underglaze-blue decorations. They seem entirely typical, yet do not recur in quantity elsewhere, suggesting the painters at Jingdezhen regularly changed the pattern books from which the porcelain designs were surely taken.

Traditional in character, the designs mostly comprise landscapes, riverscapes, scattered clusters of (carefully arranged) 'torn-off' flowers. Unlike a generation earlier, few carry figure designs. The revival of the Chinese kilns in the late seventeenth century, after decades of irregular production, coincided with the introduction, as design sources for porcelain decoration, of printed novels and romances illustrated with woodblocks of the male and female subjects.[51] Kangxi-period export porcelain is therefore often decorated with figures, more so than the later *Geldermalsen*'s cargo. It may well be that by mid-century the 'imaged' wares (as contemporary shipping and sale lists describe ceramics painted with figures) were primarily painted in enamels rather than underglaze blue. Bright overglaze colours gave more scope to create the bold panels found on many export ceramics, portraying Chinese families on terraces, warriors in entirely fantastic tournaments, or dignified officials at a multitude of professional and social activities with elegantly dressed ladies in attendance. Where the *Geldermalsen*'s cargo is painted with figural designs, the figures are normally only a small element in the overall effect; a boatman punts a tiny craft along a wide river, a solitary fisherman plies his trade.

Pl. 154. Chinese Imari Plantain pattern plate, c.1750. 23 cm diam.

The overall impression from the *Geldermalsen*'s porcelain is that underglaze-decorated human-figure subjects were not in particular demand in Europe; or, alternatively, that non-figural designs were cheaper or quicker to produce. It is surprising, therefore, that so very many contemporary European potters should have used figures in almost every pattern they painted in underglaze blue on wares which, implicitly or explicitly, were in imitation of Chinese originals.

The most striking designs found by Hatcher were on the large dishes, painted with four carp (Pl. 156). The shipping lists suggest that there should have been

Pl. 155. Underglaze-blue designs and shapes from the *Geldermalsen* cargo, c.1750.

Pl. 156. Blue and white Fish pattern dish, c.1750. 45 cm diam.

seventy-five 'fish bowls'; Hatcher's crew actually found forty-seven. They well illustrate two characteristics of Jingdezhen mass-production. One is the remarkable ability of the painters to keep on producing a complicated design apparently freehand, or using – at most – only a very simple stencil to give the broadest guide to spacing. The fish and waterweed are very similarly spaced and drawn, but, if compared closely, they are not identical. Western potters had discovered the advantages of stencil outlines by this date; rather surprisingly, there is no evidence from the cargo that the Chinese had further standardized and speeded up their pot production by learning this useful technique.

The carp dishes also show Chinese readiness to capitalize on a good design. In a number of cases, the *Geldermalsen*'s cargo includes one particular design painted on hundreds of the same kind of object, but in three different colour combinations of underglaze blue and overglaze enamels. The plain ones have, as with all the other underglaze-decorated wares, survived with the design unblemished. But the ones originally painted, more vividly, with overglaze enamels have sadly suffered. In the case of the fish dishes, those with underglaze blue forming part of the pattern still have easily recognizable fish; the ones wholly painted in overglaze enamels, where the gilding or pigment remains, mostly have only a very fragile and somewhat muddy surface decoration.

These splendid fish dishes were expensive purchases for the supercargo; a category noted as being bought for the first time in 1745, by 1746 their purchase price was 3,10 guilders. Unfortunately we do not know whether this was for the blue, or for the more expensive enamelled ones which were fired twice, the second time at a lower temperature to 'fix' the overglaze enamels. The design of these huge dishes suggests that they were always intended to lie flat on a table, for there is no one simple way in which they can be put upright on display, so that the fishes swim naturally in the same plane. The shipping invoices call them 'fish bowls', with a wide flat rim for picking them up, probably to serve some kind of prepared whole fish. They should not be confused with the wide deep tanks or cisterns, often painted inside with big fan-tailed carp, in which the Chinese once displayed their enthusiastically collected examples of ornamental fish. The carp dishes on the *Geldermalsen* were for export, and for an unequivocally culinary function.

The cargo also contained smaller saucer-dishes, with the same Fish pattern in enamels. Jorg suggests that, according to the order for 1750, the smaller ensuite ones were for butter or shrimps, though table butter would perhaps have been more appropriately contained in one of the small lidded containers which were also found. The ones recovered were unfortunately all enamelled and have not survived well, but the presumption is that they were decorated by the same workshop which manufactured and painted the larger versions.[53]

The dinner plates, over ten thousand in all, are astonishingly similar in size and proportion. Collectors have long realized that, for no apparent reason, the standard diameter of a Chinese export circular dinner plate is normally approximately 23 centimetres, with the wide, flat flange representing some 6–7 centimetres of the total width (Pls. 134, 155, 160). The *Geldermalsen* cargo shows vividly that this approximate size was indeed the norm for a Chinese export dinner plate of any pattern. The shape itself is of European, not Chinese, origin. The Chinese preferred to use saucer-dishes, curving-sided plates rather than ones with flat borders, as receptacles for food and stands, while the deep rice bowl was the basic food container at all levels of Chinese society. Where flat borders do occur on Ming and Qing ceramics, they are frequently on large, heavily potted serving dishes, often destined for foreign markets; thick, wide, celadon-glazed dishes, or massive early blue and white ones, of the type still occasionally discovered in old Indian, Iranian and Egyptian collections.

Pl. 157 (right). Blue and enamelled Fish pattern dish, c.1750. 45 cm diam.

Pl. 158 (far right). Enamelled Fish pattern dish, c.1750. 45 cm diam.

Pl. 159. Enamelled Fish pattern saucer-dishes, c.1750. 22.5 cm diam.

Pl. 160. Blue and white Boatman and Six-Flower Border pattern plates, c.1750.
23 cm diam.

Pl. 161. Blue and white Leaping Boy pattern saucer-dishes, large size, c.1750. 28.5 cm diam.
'Nests' of these blue and white saucer-dishes comprised dishes in three sizes:
28.5 cm, 25.5 cm and 23 cm diam.

Pl. 162. Massive blue and white Lotus pattern dish, mid-14th century. 44 cm diam.
It is traditionally held that these spectacular early blue and white (and also celadon) dishes
were initially developed for the export market. Many certainly appear at an early date in
Islamic and Indian kitchen inventories.

The cargo of soup plates featured only three different patterns, which is curious with so many other flatwares on board; a soup or broth course was basic to any reasonable dinner in Europe at the time, 'on the French model'. The Empty Sky pattern is unusual because of its asymmetricality, somewhat in Japanese taste (Pl. 163). Spreading across the whole lower part of the plate, it leaves a huge expanse undecorated at the top, and there is no evidence that this was ever filled with gilt or enamel decoration which has disappeared through sea immersion. More typical is the Willow Terrace pattern (Pl. 164). A willow with short thick foliage hangs over a lattice-work fence at the centre; a tall cluster of blossoming tree peony grows up beside one of the splendidly decorative 'Lake Tai' rocks. Beloved of Chinese landscape gardeners, these irregular lumps were eagerly sought for, hollowed out and eroded by currents at the bottom of the lake which gives them their name. There is no obvious reason why either of these types of soup plate should be on board. Unlike the third sort recovered, discussed as part of the Lattice Fence services, they do not match any of the other plates or shaped pieces in the cargo, and would not on the face of it have been a very desirable group to sell at the Zeeland auctions.

The Table Services

Among the varied wares contained in the 203 chests of porcelain on board, there were, according to the original shipping invoice, 171 dinner services.[54] This appears a remarkably large number, even though not all – to judge from the

Pl. 163. Blue and white Empty Sky pattern soup plate, c.1750. 23 cm diam.

Pl. 164. Blue and white Willow Terrace pattern soup plate, c.1750. 23 cm diam.

examples recovered – were decorated only in blue and white (Pls. 165, 174). They would not all have been the same size, even though the VOC records have yielded a specification in the abortive 1751 Requirements of what the VOC thought a service should include. One thinks nowadays of a large-sized Chinese export dinner service as containing 200 or more pieces; mostly dinner and soup plates, but rounded out with a variety of serving and display dishes, tureens in various sizes and smaller objects. Despite the lists of what the ideal rounded 'set' was, the *Geldermalsen*'s cargo suggests that this was by no means necessarily the case. Quite a lot can be learned from examining the actual cargo, if one bears in mind that the most regularly profitable services which the VOC imported were the relatively small ones of 50 or 120 pieces, not the massive, showy ones which can include several hundred vessels. The VOC was purchasing for a regular and non-flamboyant market in Holland.[55]

The existence of a demand for porcelain dinner sets itself reflects a significant change in Western dining arrangements since the late medieval period. Porcelain in bulk was a novel table decoration. As late as 1663, Samuel Pepys could note with genuine disapproval that a function as formal and important as the Lord Mayor's banquet at the Guildhall was furnished only with wooden plates; the City Corporation plate (silverware for official functions) had been melted down during the Civil War, and there was still no intermediate material for dining off.[56] The medieval tradition lingered; 'table service' was an action, laying a table and preparing to serve a meal, rather than the collection of vessels on which the food was placed.[57] Only in the last decades of the seventeenth century did Europe undergo what one historian has called 'a gastronomic and social revolution' in eating habits, with the development of the *dîner intime* and the unprecedented bulk availability of ceramic vessels.

The concept of dining off ceramic services seems to have developed in sixteenth-century Italy. Silver was the preferred material off which rich metropolitan families ate, but there are indications that maiolica was used on occasion as a cheaper alternative for table flatwares, especially in country villas to which aristocratic families would retire for more rustic living. Isabella d'Este certainly owned a maiolica armorial service; in the later sense of the term, it consisted of different shaped dishes and plates, each with the family arms. It was probably in Italy that wide flat border flanges, so characteristic of table plates, evolved at this date; the prototypes were on ecclesiastical gold or silver wafer plates, but many secular maiolica tablewares have this unusual form. The earliest comparable English silver ones seem to be the sets dated 1567 and 1573 in the Victoria and Albert Museum. They are heavily engraved, but apparently designed for use as well as display since they are not embossed (which would have greatly diminished their usefulness at table). Sets of usable plates survive in quantity only from after 1660.

Although more is known about traditions of British dining, the evidence suggests that there were not great differences in the development of polite dining as far afield as Scandinavia and the eastern seaboard of the American colonies. A dinner party was, by then, the main way in which the wealthier classes entertained. Feasting had traditionally been an occasion to reinforce social hierarchy, when an entire household was gathered together in a great hall. But by the eighteenth century, although there were still grand occasions in the medieval style, the notion of more private dining had developed, principally in France. A separate 'dining room' was frequently incorporated into the grand plan of a Palladian house, from which the staff would now be excluded (except as servers). By the late seventeenth century, table settings were being regularized; knives and spoons were supplemented by forks with which to eat all foods, rather than just for dainty sweetmeats as the Italians had first used their new pronged invention.[58]

Pl. 165. Part of a blue and white Lattice Fence pattern dinner service, for 144 diners, c.1750.
The normal ratio of dinner and soup plates in the 18th century would have been about three or
four dinner to one soup, to allow for the several different courses, or 'removes', which normally
included only one of a broth or stew.

Pl. 166. Famille rose part dinner service in the Sèvres taste, c.1775.
With its design specifically copying the rococo floral garlands found on table wares made at the
Sèvres factory, this service illustrates the way in which elegant dining towards the end of the
18th century required many more *pièces de forme*, serving dishes and plates than ever before.

The time at which dinner was served got later as the eighteenth century pro-
gressed, but mid-afternoon was an average time to begin the two- or three-hour
main meal of the day.[59] At the time of the English Restoration, dinner often com-
menced at midday. By the late eighteenth century, the respectable time to start
could be as late as 6 pm if one was entertaining polite company; the English man
of letters, Horace Walpole, complained at the time that he was so old-fashioned as
to dine still at 4 pm.[60] But at mid-century, the balance of daily meals was better.
Breakfast had been taken in mid-morning, often after a couple of hours' work.
The lengthy dinner lasted till early evening; a light supper, often fruit and the
remaining meat from dinner (now served cold), was available at about 7 pm,
followed by tea or coffee. (The latter was also often served after dinner.) An
observant contemporary in the early part of the century, not entirely enchanted by
the heavy midday meal, observed that 'English are gluttons at noon, and abstinent
at night'.[61] 'Luncheon' as a major meal did not become popular until the 1780s.

The changes in the time of dining coincided, over the century, with an increasing sophistication in the utensils required to serve the meal elegantly.[62] Kangxi-
period tablewares were normally dinner plates, soup plates and larger serving
dishes, often saucer-dishes at this date rather than flat-bordered ones to judge
from old inventories. A century later, the plates to furnish the main 'removes' (as
meat courses and 'sides' within a meal were called) were supplemented by pud-
ding, salad and smaller plates (Pl. 167). But entirely new elements included serving dishes with pierced removable liners, salad bowls, reticulated strainer bowls
and baskets, display bowls for fruit, small covered cups for syllabubs and custards
(made from eggs, sugar and flavourings like vanilla or cinnamon), and sauce boats
on matching shaped stands (Pl. 166). From now on, elegant porcelain figures were
supplied (primarily by Western, not Chinese, potters) to adorn lavish 'subleties',
decorative table assemblages which accompanied the serving of 'desert' (sic) and
replaced earlier démodé fanciful architectural confections of spun sugar. This extraordinary elaboration of forms within a dinner service, with pieces mostly useful

Pl. 167. The First Course Remove,
from 'Directions to set out a Table in
the most elegant manner'. Elizabeth
Raffald, *The Experienced English
Housekeeper*, 8th edition, 1782. *Private
collection.*

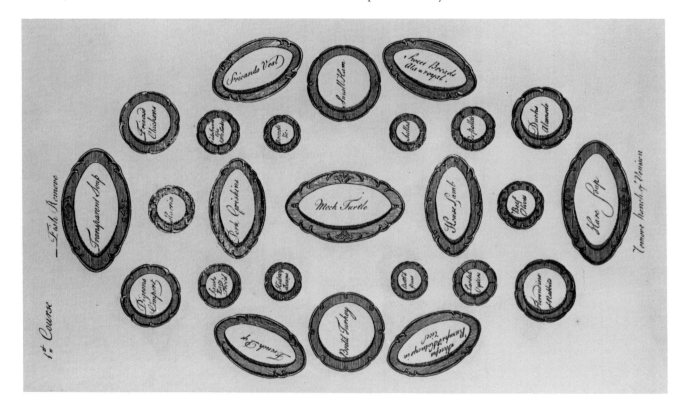

Pl. 168. Blue and white Fruiting Vine pattern oval tureen, cover and stand, c.1750.

The Fruiting Vine pattern is rare on export blue and white porcelain of mid-century date, though it occurs more frequently on large dishes of late Kangxi date. The only other wares with this pattern discovered on the *Geldermalsen* were three dishes, 41 cm wide, two other tureens and a few plates; this suggests that there was at least one full service on board.

but often almost concealed by a baroque or rococo sculptural exuberance, owed much to the porcelain designers at Meissen, adapting free-standing figural design to the requirements of the modern dinner table.

Tureens and covers by now came in a variety of shapes (Pl. 168). The largest were to serve soups, stews or broths; the latter, often preferred to thinner, clearer soups, were made from the reduced stock when a joint had been boiled rather than roasted for dinner.[63] The smaller ones are normally identified as sauce tureens, and when covered would certainly diminish the speed at which sauces would cool or thicken. Contrary to popular belief, sauces were often not vastly spicy and original. Visitors to Britain noted that one of four basic kinds sufficed to enhance most dinner courses, the choice being bread sauce for fowl and game, apple sauce with duck and pork, fennel sauce with fish, and an ubiquitous white or butter sauce for most other forms of flesh.[64] Food was not elaborate except in the highest circles, and this was a level of society for which the porcelain contents of the *Geldermalsen*'s commercial cargo were not destined. Nutrition was available in generous quantities, but cooked simply; the meat roast or boiled, the fish baked, the vegetables well-cooked. Traditionally, medical men were thought to disapprove of the eating of raw vegetables, but this was clearly an old-fashioned opinion by the time of the *Geldermalsen*; many dinner services have references to salad bowls as essential vessels required.[65] A balanced meal was regarded as being in four parts: a first and second 'remove', a salad and cheese course, and a more elaborate 'desert' course, sometimes served in a different room altogether; the salad was a basic element of this structure.

The *Geldermalsen*'s services were very uneven in variety of shapes and number of pieces. Intended for purchasers at different social levels, the imbalance may have been worsened by the losses when the ship sank. But the 1751 Requirements specify clearly what the VOC had wanted a service to comprise: fifteen serving dishes (one of 36 centimetres, two of 32 centimetres, four of 28 centimetres, and eight of 25.5 centimetres); eight circular salad bowls of 25.5 centimetres diameter, and two octagonal; twelve dishes of 23 centimetres, twelve of 20.5 centimetres;

100 dinner plates (assuredly of 23 centimetres); four candlesticks, four salt cellars, two butter dishes, and two sauce boats.[66] The lack of any mention of tureens is inexplicable. In other itemized services located by Jorg, such as the ones shipped in 1750, a service of forty-seven pieces, with twenty soup and twenty dinner plates, would have had one large and one small tureen; while a 'set' of eighty-four pieces would have had not merely two tureens, but also four salt cellars and sauce boats, and eight fruit dishes. For simpler dining, services ordered in 1750 comprised twenty-five pieces (plates and serving dishes only); an intermediate service of sixty-nine pieces was also shipped.[67] Clearly there was no fixed size; the retail 'Chinamen' in Europe assembled sets, as required by clients, from the huge lots bought uneventfully for stock year after year at the annual Company wholesale auctions. The range of vessels required for a complete service increased throughout the eighteenth century; the VOC regarded a full service in c. 1780 as consisting of 462 pieces, and they could even be as extensive as the services in 1766 which comprised *in toto* 631 vessels.[68]

But most were far smaller. The Co-Hong merchant Sweetia supplied to the British ship *Prince George* in September 1755 an order of 'seven table sets, blue and white, octagon [-al]', as follows: 'two tureens, covers and stands; thirteen dishes in various sizes; sixty dinner plates; twenty-four soup plates; eight salad dishes; one salad bowl; two sauce boats; four salts'. A set of this composition cost 15 taels, or £5.[69] A notable Chinese blue and white 'table service' was presumably new (or only slightly secondhand) when it went under James Christie's hammer in Pall Mall in July 1767. The different balance of pieces that the vendor-owner had originally chosen was obviously for less elaborate dining. There was one tureen, cover and stand, for stew or soup; two smaller ditto, presumably for sauces or vegetables; sixteen oblong dishes, and eight various (this suggests they were circular saucer-dishes, possibly deeper for salad), seventy-four plates, twelve soup plates, four sauce boats, and four salts. The disproportionate number of dinner plates to soup plates is perplexing; one soup course and six other 'removes' was not a normal balance.

The *Geldermalsen* yielded only four patterns of wares that could be confidently identified as belonging originally to services or 'sets', since in each case there were different shapes and sizes of wares with the same pattern. Much the most striking was the Lattice Fence design. Only in the case of this pattern had the VOC supercargoes managed to find sufficient numbers of shaped pieces at Canton to enable large, potentially rounded services to be assembled; and thousands of them survived, in impeccable condition. Taking a tip from eighteenth-century 'Chinamen', Christie's made up the heterogeneous remaining group of Lattice Fence wares into a number of services, to seat dinner parties from twelve guests up to 144. This latter spectacular assemblage of 380 pieces of porcelain in pristine condition was probably the biggest service ever offered at auction by Christie's, in over two centuries of continuous fine art auctioneering. The excitement when it came under the hammer set the seal on the quite remarkable *Geldermalsen* sale. It sold for £219,460; this was then the highest price ever achieved at auction, anywhere, for a porcelain dinner service.

Among the Lattice Fence shaped pieces, the circular tureens, salts and small, footed containers with covers caused great interest. It is always claimed that many of these types of object are directly copied from European silver originals.[70] Trying to identify the contemporary silver vessels which should have formed very similar prototypes has proved surprisingly difficult, leading to the unexpected conclusion that the tureen shapes do not closely follow the more standard examples current at that date in precious metal (Pl. 170). Silver tureens of the decades around the time of the *Geldermalsen*, for example, would almost invariably

Pl. 169. Blue and white Lattice Fence pattern dish, c.1750. 42 cm diam.

Pl. 170. Two blue and white Lattice
Fence pattern circular tureens and
covers, c.1750. 23.5 cm wide.

Pl. 171 (opposite page, top). Six blue
and white Lattice Fence pattern lobed
waisted salts, c.1750. 8.5 cm wide.

Pl. 172 (opposite page, below). Two
blue and white Lattice Fence pattern
condiment jars and covers, c.1750.
11.5 cm wide.

have been of oval *bombe* form, rather than circular. Flat, half-flower-head tureen handles, of the type discovered by Hatcher on Lattice Fence tureens and known from many other export wares, are apparently unknown on silver of this date; rococo scrolling, or shell-form, ones are the normal applied fixtures.

The octagonal salts are equally confusing (Pl. 171). Although waisted circular upright salts occur in silver, the line of the top rim is normally flat-faceted, to match the eight sides of the waist, rather than scalloped outwards, as the *Geldermalsen*'s are. At this mid-century date, anyway, silver salts were normally flatter, octagonal or oval-shaped 'trencher' recessed types rather than upright pedestal ones. Upright porcelain salts are found earlier in famille verte and Japanese *kakiemon* ceramics, all datable to much nearer 1700 AD.[71] The closest prototype may be Dutch pewter upright salts of the early seventeenth century.

Salts indicate how dining in company was changing. The age of the elaborate medieval standing salt, establishing hierarchy, was over. No longer was a guest honoured, or humiliated, by his host as he sat down to dine respectively 'above' or 'below' the salt, placed at a strategic point on the table where it socially differentiated the guests.[72] Less formal eating required smaller recessed 'trencher' salts of precious and coarse metals, pottery and porcelain. Several diners would share a single salt; the 'Prince George' order suggests four salts would be required for twelve diners.

The Lattice Fence covered jars on short stem feet are very unusual (Pl. 172). The VOC lists do not mention their purpose, but they most likely contained dry powdered spices or mustard. There is no aperture in the rim of the shallow lid to accommodate the shaft of a spoon or ladle (such as one finds with earlier mustard pots or on some contemporary sauce and soup tureens), so diners took a pinch by hand, spoon or knife-tip, like salt. The 'unpacking books' for 1749 mention two mustard pots as part of a service of 110 pieces. As Jorg notes, Hatcher's discovery of fifty-six of these pots should mean that there was a potential for at least twenty-eight Lattice Fence services of 110 pieces in the *Geldermalsen* cargo.[73]

The second service had one of the ship's most striking designs, the Zigzag

Pl. 173. Blue and white Zigzag Fence pattern dishes and plates, c.1750. Dishes 39 cm diam, plates
23 cm diam.

Pl. 174. Blue and gilt Three Pavilions pattern part service, c.1750. Dishes 39.5, 36, 32 and 29 cm diam, plates 23 cm diam, soup plates 22.5 cm diam.

Fence pattern, painted in an unusually strong blue, of violet tone, which gave a particular boldness to the larger dishes (Pl. 173). Hatcher found no standing vessels or *pièces de forme* at all with the Zigzag Fence pattern, suggesting it was a small service from current stock. Otherwise typical of Jingdezhen riverscape designs, the Zigzag Fence was unusual in having a well-drawn, and very visible, boatman poling his punt (with a thatched canopy) across the right-hand side of the centre, which depicted a wide tranquil river lapping at the bank of a pine terrace.

The third service was the only one to have decoration over the glaze also, gilding which was always intended to be an integral part of the design; the pattern was incomplete where it had disappeared (Pl. 174). Thus it was planned as more than a mere enhancement of a line or a border, the way gilding was usually applied on European ceramics (apart from the confections of independent outside-gilders like the Auffenwerth *hausmalern* at Augsburg). This particular category of service was unusual because it consisted only of plates, shallow and deep dishes, all moulded with brown-dressed barbed rims.

The fourth service is known only by a few isolated octagonal matching table pieces, of typical mid-century type. By an accident of packing, which meant that very few examples of it survived, this fourth service pattern is known mainly from a matching group of fifty-seven round butter dishes, and twenty sauce boats which seem to be related to them by virtue of the broadly similar design and the trellis border (Pls. 3, 178, 181). The extant flatwares are only a deep dish, an incomplete serving dish and several plates. They are all painted with a rather packed scene, incorporating two figures crossing a stone-walled bridge towards a tiered small pavilion and two thatched retreats standing on stilts at the water's edge.

The shipping list recorded that there should be 171 services in the cargo of 203 crates of porcelain.[74] It is a great pity that we are not able to identify more precisely the composition and variety of the services that represent, when seen as a group together, the most striking ceramics recovered from the wreck.

Vessels of Western Inspiration

The *Geldermalsen* carried among its Company purchases some unusually shaped porcelains. As the porcelain trade between China and Europe revived from the very end of the seventeenth century, one of the more interesting innovations was the system whereby porcelain-buying Westerners could commission not just specially painted designs, such as coats-of-arms, but also specially potted shapes which have no place in the Chinese domestic ceramic tradition. The Dutch were commissioning wares from Japan in the middle of the seventeenth century, but the next century saw an expansion of this useful system as Chinese trade through Canton settled into a regular annual pattern. Western-manufactured models in wood, metal and ceramics (like Dutch Delft) were sent out to Canton. Dropped off at Jingdezhen by Chinese merchants on their way north to the major business and gold-dealing centre at Nanjing, the wares were potted in as close an imitation of the original as the Chinese could achieve, and then returned by coastwise and overland routes to Canton in time for the next trading season. Hatcher found a number of shapes which must have been commissioned and delivered in this manner, to fit the particular requirements of one of the Western Companies. No doubt, if the product sold well and could be produced profitably, the potter who had developed it would continue production.

Such seems to have been the case with a category of handled bowls, which were initially thought to be chamber pots for children (Pl. 175). The archives revealed

Pl. 175. Two blue and white vomit pots, c.1750. 15.5 cm wide. Although the 'Requirements' for the returning cargo from Canton specifically prohibited their purchase, these invalid bowls were bought decorated in all three standard palettes – blue, blue and enamels, and enamels only.

their real function. During the late 1740s, the VOC had taken delivery each year of 'vomit pots' (*spuijgpotjes*); demand had decreased in Holland, although they were shipped for five years until 1751, in which year the 'Requirements for the Return Cargoes' specifically instructed that none should be purchased that season.[75] Earlier Requirements referred to them originally as handled sickness bowls, modelled in the manner of small water pots or chamber pots for children. They were painted, like the carp dishes, in the three different combinations of blue and enamels. These vessels were not a substantial part of a VOC commercial cargo. With fragile rims and wide delicate handles, they required careful packing and a volume of freight space probably unjustified by profitability as their auction price in Holland declined. Jorg suggested that larger chamber pots, which were purchased over a much longer period, were easier to buy because they would come from regular stock in Canton,[76] even if less convenient to pack, with larger handles. Perhaps small objects were packed inside. Most of the few large ones recovered have marine encrustation or glaze erosion, suggesting they were bought late in the season and stacked right at the top of the hold. The smaller ones could at least be tightly packed with other things jammed around them; Hatcher's underwater film shows three, wedged one above the other in the original shallow wooden crate where they divided horizontal stacks of simple bowls.

Butter tubs and covers were found on the *Geldermalsen* in two shapes, circular and oval (Pls. 176, 177). Circular ones had appeared in earlier shipping Requirements, until 1745 accompanied by matching saucers; oval ones, which came without saucers, appeared only in the lists from 1750, showing that this sort would have been a novelty in Europe if they had arrived.[77] The shape is ultimately derived from wooden containers; the functionless horizontal ribs at the upper edge and foot rim imitate the fibrous bands holding the planked wooden domestic vessels together. This origin explains, too, the unusual low pierced bracket forming the long finial on the covers of six of the seven types of butter tub recovered. The original wooden tubs would have been fitted with a large bracket handle,

Pl. 176. Two blue and white oval tubs and covers, c.1750. 11.5 cm wide.

Pl. 177. Two blue and white circular butter tubs and covers, c.1750. 11.5 cm wide.

Pl. 178. Two blue and white circular butter tubs and covers, c.1750. 11.5 cm diam.
These are clearly to be associated with the few surviving pieces, mostly octagonal, from a service painted with two travellers crossing a bridge towards a group of pavilions. The design on the top matches exactly, but the main design on the sides is completely different; the only match in the cargo is a group of sauceboats, otherwise barely related, which do admittedly have trellis pattern borders.

fitting at both sides of the rim into vertical brackets to retain a flat cover. The porcelain versions have the bracket attached directly to the cover, and the two side handles now have no purpose. The underwater film shows that each tub was packed with its cover upside down on top, so that the bracket handle was protected by the body of the tub; unfortunately many of the very fragile side handles had been broken.

The two shapes of butter tub – round and oval – were each painted with the same pattern in three different palettes: underglaze blue, blue and enamels, and enamels only. There was one different category of butter tub. Circular, and painted only in blue, these had a simple 'flowerbud' finial on the cover and an attractive design, which closely matched that on the few objects remaining from the octagonal dinner service (Pl. 178). Jorg suggested that these tubs may have formed part of this category of service. If so, this might explain why, unusually, the packing lists recorded less than were actually recovered. There were fifty-seven of these 'flowerbud-finial' tubs; the lists showed that there should have been 195 single butter dishes (i.e. individual objects, not part of a service), and Hatcher found a total of 253.[78]

Cylindrical beer tankards follow what the VOC regarded as an English form.[79] Straight-sided with strong loop handles, they were supplied only in the 'Chinees-Japans' (Chinese Imari) palette (Pl. 179). The Requirements for 1750 stressed that they should not have covers, the unstated reason being that Europeans had long themselves fitted hinged pewter, silver or wood covers onto the locally made tankards, flagons and steins. For the 1751 trading season, mugs had been requested in four sizes of capacity, and in the usual three palettes rather than just Chinese Imari as the year before. The supercargoes in fact ended up with mugs in only three sizes, one pint, one and a half pint, and two pint; and, judging by the survivors, the Heren XVII would have received none at all in underglaze blue only, or enamels only, such as they had said they also wanted.[80]

There were three kinds of sauce boat in the cargo, but surprisingly none which

Pl. 179. Two blue and enamelled cylindrical tankards, c.1750. 13.5 cm high.

completely matched the Lattice Fence pattern. One type, of which forty-five were recovered, could well have been intended as part of the Lattice Fence complement (Pl. 180); even though the decoration is only floral, the geometric border design matches that on the salts and spice pots.[81] Using the same reasoning, it is possible that the twenty boats decorated with bamboo and pine were intended as part of the octagonal services, since their side patterns match the sides of the 'odd' butter tubs with flower finials.[82] Sauce boats should certainly have been included as part of the larger services in this pattern; but, of course, they may have been lost in the wreck.

The ones recovered are all of similar proportion and of Western metal inspiration. All have a pronounced rounded bulge rising vertically from the rim at both sides of the handle, and a smaller sharp point nearer the drawn-out spout. All stand somewhat low to the ground, distinguished in shipping Requirements of the period as sauce boats with hollow feet, rather than with flat bases directly on the ground.[83] As with the tureen, the shape has been universally (but erroneously) accepted as a derivation of a standard contemporary silver shape. The irregularly shaped rim occurs very often on Chinese export sauce boats of mid-eighteenth-century date, but in fact it is exceptionally rare to find it on contemporary European silver. It remains to be discovered which particular European silver-smith, or VOC designer, created the original sauce boat for a generation of Chinese export copies. Sauce boats in silver were an innovation of the 1720s, but the earliest ones have spouts at both ends of the oval bodies, and handles on both sides. By about 1740, they had become single-handled and spouted, but, rather than standing on oval, plain bases, almost all had now acquired three separate small feet as supports.[84]

Chinese export spittoons are not normally found in early European inventories, and the *Geldermalsen* seems to have been carrying a remarkably large group for a market where they were less essential a part of domestic life than in South Asia (Pl. 184). The shape was inconvenient to transport; the wide, thin flange made a

Pl. 180. Two blue and white Flowering Shrubs pattern sauce boats, c. 1750. 21 cm wide.

Pl. 181. Two blue and white Pine and Bamboo pattern sauce boats, c. 1750. 21 cm wide.

spittoon very fragile, and those with wide handles (the enamelled variety) required even more freight space than the handleless majority. *Quispedoren* were bought with some regularity from 1737, and they formed part of nearly every cargo from 1764.[85] Despite increasing availibility, few seem to have survived in Europe; fragile and not well balanced, they must have been extremely vulnerable. The handleless ones were painted with floral meanders in the standard three variations of blue and enamels; the handled ones, slightly taller, were painted only with a more elaborate floral enamel decoration.

Milk bowls, steep-sided bowls with a large loop handle and a small 'beak' spout at right angles to it, appeared in VOC shipping records from 1745.[86] The shape is unprecedented in Chinese export, but prototype jugs exist in silver; West Country English silversmiths were making them in Exeter at about this date (Pl. 183). The metal versions would probably have been more convenient, because porcelain ones are fairly ungainly when full.[87] Jorg suggested that they might be for dipping bread into milk, to eat from;[88] or they could have served to skim the cream off milk in Europe and America (where they were certainly made for dairy purposes). Being in two sizes, two pints and half a pint, the smaller could have been used as feeding bowls for invalids, in the manner of porringers or posset pots.

Several bottles found on Hatcher's last visit were of the type used in the West as water bottles to accompany deep basins (Pl. 182). They appear in English shipping invoices as 'guglets', from the French *gorgelets*.[89] These globular (or sometimes faceted) bottles have tall, narrow necks, with often a small globe at the top of the neck just below a flaring rim; this globe must have produced a gurgling effect, unconsciously reflected in the name! Only one (encrusted) companion basin was found; the type and shape is fairly new in Chinese export and clearly regarded as useful, since many English soft-paste porcelain factories produced 'guglets and basons' from an early date.[90] Maybe the Western market preferred slightly more luxurious versions than blue and white, because Chinese ones are most commonly

Pl. 182. Two blue and white globular water bottles ('guglets'), c.1750. 25.5 cm high.

Pl. 183. Two blue and white milk jugs, large and small size, c.1750. 21 cm and 17.5 cm wide.

Pl. 184. Two blue and white Chrysanthemum Scroll pattern spittoons, c.1750. 12.6 cm diam.

found enamelled. The Dutch only bought these water bottles, to accompany washing basins, until 1760.[91]

Several tureens of oblong octagonal and oval form were found, mostly covered in marine growths (Pl. 168). Probably they were not part of the Company's purchases, deep in the hold; the thirty or more Company-owned Lattice Fence tureens and covers were in impeccable condition, the glaze shiny and entirely uneroded. No dishes or plates with the same designs as these tureens were recovered, suggesting they did not come from complete services. They were most likely bought as 'private cargo' from current stock in Canton at the end of the trip, and tucked into one of the ship's numerous cubby-holes, for personal use or resale in the West. Hatcher found another badly degraded table ornament which, too,

was almost certainly 'private trade'. This was a square stand with four apertures on top in two different sizes; a 'trame' (as the metal originals were called) to hold oil and vinegar bottles and small containers of spice, pepper, salt, or even sugar, shakers. The VOC asked for some sets including containers for oil, vinegar, mustard and pepper to be sent as rather expensive Company purchases in 1764, but these stood on a wide flat base rather than in frames.[92]

The last category of Western-inspired vessels present in any quantity was tea pots, in two basic shapes. A total of 522 were recovered; very few, given the vast number of tea and coffee bowls. But the shipping invoices noted that only 578 were packed, so it was not the case that thousands were lost during the shipwreck.[93] The VOC Requirements had reached Canton too late to be acted on. Did the supercargoes know of a glut in the European market?[94] That seems unlikely. The small number of tea pots could be simply because other supercargoes had bought up the stocks available, or a consignment from Jingdezhen had failed to arrive in time. There must have been many such trading problems and bottlenecks. The early years did have certain advantages, when supercargoes could contract simply for '25 to 30 tons of china-ware – the ordinary sort, viz. dishes, plates and bowls', and not have to worry about the precise composition.[95]

Of the two basic shapes, the simpler version, painted in the three standard colour schemes, has a globular body, pronounced neck and flat rim, wide, simple loop handle and straight spout; the cover is shallowly domed, and has a flowerbud finial (Pl. 185). All five of the shapes carry similar designs, not identical, but clearly related; the main element is a fenced terrace of peony and willow at the right, and there is a band of Trellis pattern enclosing the aperture for the cover. The more striking version is characterized by a splendid curved handle of T-shape (Pl. 186). The baluster body of the pot narrows to the base, in a proportion silver collectors call 'bullet-shaped'; the almost-flat top is recessed for a small matching cover with tapering finial. The fragile handle derives from Western metalwork, but, when found in English silver, it often dates to the 1720s and 1730s; once again, the prototype well antedates the *Geldermalsen*.[96] The handle seems to have its closest parallel in German porcelain of the second quarter of the century, particularly on the products of the Meissen factory in Saxony. There is no Imari version of these bullet-shaped tea pots; the fifty-six tea pots missing from the original total may well be largely this group, packed in a more vulnerable area of the hold.

Tea pots are almost invariably associated with tea sets. The shipping documents mention no other elements of a tea set in the cargo (apart, of course, from the tea bowls, chocolate and coffee cups); but this was a five-year period, 1745–50, during which the VOC inexplicably bought no fully composed tea sets. We can now extend the period to 1751. A tea set would normally also require a slop bowl, milk jug, one (or two) tea caddies, sugar bowl (for cut or ground cane sugar) and a spoon tray. The *Geldermalsen* carried none of these as Company wares, although a few of the accessories that one would expect were recovered in an extremely eroded condition: egg-shaped tea caddies, pear-shaped cream jugs and several spoon trays (both in hard paste and the less commonly found soft paste, a beige-coloured, lower-fired variant of normal Chinese porcelain), all presumably isolated 'private cargo'.

The Bowls

After the tea and coffee wares, bowls formed the second largest element in the cargo; some 25,921 were loaded originally.[97] The range of designs on the thousands recovered is extremely limited, dividing into only about four different

Pl. 185. Two blue and white globular tea pots and covers, c.1750. 21 cm wide.

Pl. 186. Two blue and white 'bullet-shaped' tea pots and covers, c. 1750. 22.5 cm wide.

Pl. 187. Blue and white Scholar on Bridge pattern bowls, c.1750. 15 cm diam.

designs, although three are available in different sizes and palettes. Three have some underglaze blue in the design. It is possible that the missing 9,000 mostly comprised more expensive ones decorated with bright enamels, but it is surprising to have found only a very few examples of this type among the thousands successfully recovered. The invoice calls them slop bowls (*spoelkommen*), although none appear to match the tea sets, so they were not meant to accompany the tea wares; presumably they were purely kitchen crockery.

Four types of bowl were purchased with the Scholar on Bridge pattern; each shows a solitary figure on a bridge approaching a pavilion nestling beneath pine (Pls. 187, 188). The larger quantity were in blue and white, in two sizes (19 and 15 centimetres diameter); the smaller in what was a variety of 'Chinees-Japans', with an extra unidentifiable enamel on the tree leaves, also available in two sizes (19 and 16.5 centimetres diameter).

There was only one other enamelled bowl recovered in large numbers, and this too was in 'Chinese Imari' palette (Pl. 189). It had the design of a tree peony cluster in blossom, beside a landscape gardener's tall ornamental pierced rock; a lattice-work fence, as so often in Jingdezhen designs, encloses the terrace scattered with shrubs and small leafy trees. The brown 'dressing' along the rim, very much a feature of Japanese ceramics (notably *kakiemon*) at an earlier date, derived in fact from a late Ming Chinese technique developed initially to help stabilize the rather brittle glaze along the vulnerable edge of smaller vessels; later it served as a base to 'fix' rim gilding.

Perhaps most historically interesting were the 'Batavian ware' bowls. Like the 'Batavian' coffee cups, these are decorated with a brown glaze washed over the whole exterior, although the area within the foot is left white. Inside, the bowl has a design in underglaze blue at the centre, and another around the well. Found with two patterns, one is a simple design of three sprays of leafy peony on two sizes of bowl (19 centimetres and 16.5 centimetres diameter); the other a riverscape around half the interior in only one size (15 centimetres diameter) (Pl. 190).

The large quantity of bowls (and coffee cups) with brown-glazed exteriors is a

Pl. 188. Blue and enamelled Scholar on Bridge pattern bowl, c.1750. 15 cm diam.

Pl. 189. Chinese Imari Peony Rock pattern bowl, c. 1750. 15 cm diam.

Pl. 190. Brown-glazed blue and white Batavian Landscape pattern bowls, c.1750. 15 cm diam.

Pl. 191. Brown-glazed blue and white Batavian Floral pattern bowls, c.1750. 19 cm diam.
The smaller bowls of this design were 16.5 cm diam.

striking feature of the *Geldermalsen*'s cargo. Before the ship was identified, these brown-glazed bowls were a valuable tool in establishing its approximate date. They are surprisingly uncommon in Europe, despite the large numbers on board. The *Geldermalsen*'s quantity may have been atypical; however, another documentary cargo contained 'Batavian' wares in large numbers. They were on the *Gotheborg*, a Swedish East India Company ship which sank right at the end of its return journey on 12 September 1745, as it entered the Swedish harbour of the same name, headquarters of the Swedish East India Company.[98] The ship was soon investigated by divers trying to salvage cargo, and brown-glazed bowls were recovered from it in some considerable numbers; they were being offered at auction from 'old' collections as early as 1893.[99] Like the coffee cups, these 'Batavian' bowls are not high-quality merchandise and few have survived elsewhere. Were they therefore popular only for a few years? The palette derives from those earlier famille verte wares which have pale brown exteriors, in which guise they influenced early European potters (such as those at Meissen) looking for appealing wares to copy.[100] The 'Batavian' bowls and coffee cups on the *Geldermalsen* are thickly potted, in contrast with the other thinner cups on board painted only in blue and white. Were all these types of coarse 'brown' wares, the coffee cups and the bowls which could well have served as slop bowls, destined for commercial use in Europe, rather than private homes? The survival rate in social clubs, coffee houses and inns would probably have been much less than in home use.

Only one design appeared in any substantial quantities on sets of bowls with matching under-dishes: the Flying Geese pattern, a subject beloved of the Chinese (Pl. 192). The wide riverscape stretches right across the saucer; in the foreground, a solitary figure crouches fishing from a small boat, and the water's surface is broken by several of the mysterious, partially submerged, rocks which one English porcelain decorator exaggerated so much that collectors have christened him the 'cannonball painter'. The depiction of the flight of geese well shows that each piece is hand-drawn, although produced as a mass order; the flights range in

Pl. 192. Blue and white Flying Geese pattern bowls and saucer-dishes, c.1750. Bowls 11.5 cm diam, saucer-dishes 17.5 cm diam.

shape from a precise V-shape to an almost straight line, though the balance of the design's elements remains constant.

Hatcher found few examples of the only other design which appears on bowls with matching saucers. The wide bowl had a simple incised flowerhead band dividing two narrower bands of blue trellis pattern, under a standard thin, clear glaze. The group is interesting, because a number of these export wares which combine underglaze-blue trellis borders with a wide band of incised foliage are known over-enamelled (probably in Holland) with a scene from a Western print resembling depictions of the Italian Commedia dell'Arte.

Pl. 193. Blue and white Floral Lappet
pattern bowl, c.1750. 15 cm diam.
Not made for the European market,
these had an unglazed ring inside,
to allow several to be stacked upright.

Pl. 194. Blue and white Scrolling Peony pattern
bowl, c.1750. 15 cm diam.
These were glazed all over the interior, with no
central ring reserved in the biscuit for kiln-stacking,
as on the bowls opposite.

Pl. 195. Blue and white Flower Spray pattern
saucer-dish, c.1750. 18.5 cm diam.
Also intended for export to the Indonesian archipelago
or farther westwards, this type has again a distinctive
unglazed 'annulet' or ring around the centre.

Pl. 196. Blue and white 'Chi' dragon saucer-dish,
c.1750. 19.5 cm diam.
The young 'Chi' dragon, here seen amongst
cloud-scrolls, is distinguished from its older relation
by the fact that it has clawless pad feet.

The cargo of bowls contributes one final detail to our knowledge of export market ceramics. The *Geldermalsen* carried a large group of rather coarse blue and white bowls, painted with two closely similar floral designs (Pls. 193, 194). The coarse body and design associated them with two types of shallow saucer-dish, roughly painted in a greyish-blue tone (Pls. 195, 196). Recent excavations have found similar wares at sites near Hong Kong, and they are certainly southern Chinese provincial export ceramics, not Jingdezhen products. This sort of material was not imported to Europe, except perhaps when Westerners returned from the East. It never features in early European inventories, because it was coarse even by contemporary Western standards of domestic 'crocks'. Logically it was not coming as Company cargo to Europe; and there was too much to be a 'private cargo'. The ship was neither destined to those South Asian ports where such coarse crockery had long been sold, via the Chinese junk trade to Batavia, nor stopping at Batavia to unload goods; the cargo and crew was at last on the direct route home to Europe. There was only one point where the ship would stop for a considerable period to reprovision, do running repairs, and to sample the considerable comforts of a well-equipped and long-established vital Dutch 'factory'. This stopping-point, at the Cape of Good Hope, boasted – as William Hickey discovered and noted in 1780 – a magnificent garden, excellent food and wine, and opportunities to stretch your legs, cramped after sea travel, with an exhausting scramble up Table Mountain, where a band and lavish picnic waited to greet a successful climber. The *Geldermalsen*'s cargo of coarse south Chinese stonewares, intended for the Cape, suggests that the entertainment may have been outstanding, but the crockery was not much to enthuse over, if Jorg's identification is correct.[101] The 'factory' asked Batavia in Spring 1751 to supply 2,000 plates, 600 serving dishes, medium size, 200 large bowls and 400 smaller ones; what Hatcher found was the remaining core of the order.[102] Much was in poor condition, the surface abraded or encrusted with marine life; the result of being stored deliberately high in the ship, accessible for unloading in Table Bay, the Cape anchorage some three hours' journey from the 'factory' complex (Pl. 197).

Pl. 197. Thomas Whitcombe. A convoy of English East India merchant ships entering Table Bay. Signed and dated 1817. 92.7 × 138.4 cm.
The Cape provided a welcome safe anchorage and source of fresh fruit and vegetables to East Indiamen all year round, though it was exceedingly hazardous to try to pass round the Cape of Good Hope under sail during the stormy winter months.

The packing lists mention two large crates containing unlisted private purchases by senior ship's crew addressed to individuals in the Netherlands. They may have included those 'private trade' ceramics which have no parallels in the Company cargo. Among the presumed private purchases, there were parts of two garnitures of five vases, three baluster-shaped with covers and, as usual with five-piece garnitures, two of beaker shape; the enamel decoration has entirely disappeared, and the 'ghosting' which one can sometimes see when enamels have gone gives no help in discovering the original design. Perhaps they were decorated with even more fragile gilding. There were single jars and covers, of oviform shape and standard export quality, painted in underglaze blue with large medallions of lotus blooms suspending pairs of symmetrical leaf sprays above and below; the type is normally dated to the earlier eighteenth century. A group of small encrusted blue and white tea bowls and saucers with facetted sides and scalloped rims was also a surprising find; the shape is more characteristic of a date twenty years earlier, for these delicate, thinly finished tea wares are often found painted with figures in Yongzheng-period rose-verte enamels.[103] Rare objects like the small group of now-datable Yixing brown stoneware teapots were almost certainly 'private trade' (Pl. 198). But the two large crates which are recorded as containing personal purchases must also have contained 'private trade' goods more expensive than porcelain. Many of the surviving ceramic oddments suggest that they originally formed parts of sets, even in one case a dinner service, and must therefore have been Company cargo, because the original quantities would have exceeded the capacity of two very spacious chests. Others may well have served as domestic crockery on board. Martabans, for example, had been used for centuries on the inter-Asiatic shipping routes to contain perishable foodstuffs like rice and grain. Hatcher's discovery of fifty-three shows that, even if old, they were still in use as late as 1750; valuable evidence, since they are often dated unequivocally to the Ming period.

Pl. 198. Four Yixing brown stoneware tea pots, c.1750. 16.5–22.5 cm wide. Very few Yixing wares were found in the wreck. They may well have been 'private cargo' because they were, like other 'personal' purchases, rather encrusted with marine growths, suggesting storage high up in the hold. Imported Yixing brown stonewares, especially tea pots, were an important source of inspiration for early European potters, particularly in England and Germany.

Pl. 199. Fifteen various olive- and brown-glazed storage jars. Before 1750, probably first half of
the 18th century.
These jars are called 'martabans' in the ceramic literature, and were used as heavy-duty
containers to ship staple foods and oils around the archipelago.

Pl. 200. Three glazed models of the 'Tyrolean (or Peasant) Dancers', c.1750. 16 and 15 cm ht.

Pl. 201. Eleven various white-glazed Daoist Immortals, a model of a recumbent lady, and a
fragmentary group of Shoulao riding a stag, c.1750. Immortals c.10 cm ht.

One group of wares must surely have been 'private trade' purchases; the small figure models – humans, birds and animals. The VOC was very unenthusiastic about purchasing figures, although it would do so occasionally. In 1746, it sent out Delftware models of cows to have copied as 120 Chinese pairs for sale in Holland.[104] The European market for Chinese figure models had declined substantially; fifty year earlier, the English East India Company was annually importing thousands of figures, mostly blanc-de-chine. The growth of a European ceramic industry had caused the decline; there was still a big mid-century market in Europe for figures, and in Holland standing figures and groups (made in Delft of tin-glazed earthenware) are some of the most endearing productions of the native eighteenth-century kilns. The Dutch market in mid-century was perhaps less hungry for brightly enamelled China trade figures than buyers in England, France or Denmark (an unexpectedly active market for 'mannikins' as noted in 1738).[105] Chinese export figures are less commonly found in early inventories of Dutch houses than in English or French ones, where they were often set into elaborate ormolu mounts. Previous VOC Requirements do not lead us to expect any figures on board; the poor physical condition of many discovered by Hatcher suggests that they were in 'private trade' boxes up near the decks.

Very few of the figures give the impression of having at one time been enamelled; those that do have been uniformly degraded by the sea to a matt biscuit surface. This is a pity, because two models are of considerable interest. Nothing more evokes the spirit of the Chinese copying what was – for them – a meaningless original model, than the fragmentary remains of five groups reproducing in Jingdezhen porcelain a Meissen group known as the 'Tyrolean' or 'peasant' dancers (Pl. 200). This very distinctive rococo group was first modelled by J.F. Eberlein in 1735 at the Meissen factory, lavishly financed from its inception by its patron and moving spirit, the Elector of Saxony, Augustus II ('the Strong'). The modeller was one of several superb sculptors who gave the factory its unparalleled reputation for a wide variety of splendidly frivolous figures and groups, each

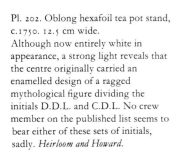

Pl. 202. Oblong hexafoil tea pot stand, c.1750. 12.5 cm wide. Although now entirely white in appearance, a strong light reveals that the centre originally carried an enamelled design of a ragged mythological figure dividing the initials D.D.L. and C.D.L. No crew member on the published list seems to bear either of these sets of initials, sadly. *Heirloom and Howard.*

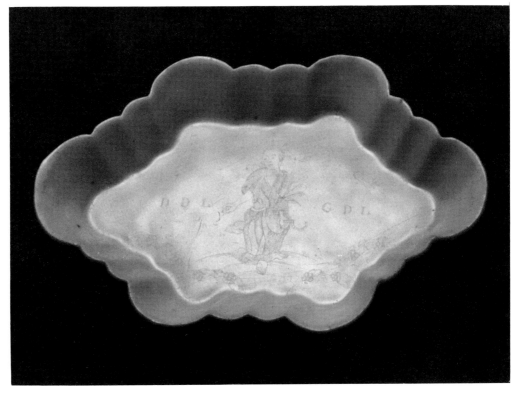

assembled from piece-moulded elements by 'repairers' (Pl. 203). The Meissen original must presumably have been taken to Jingdezhen for careful copying there, so it can have arrived at Canton at the latest during the trading season of 1749 or 1750; it could well have been earlier, if the first Chinese efforts to reproduce this elaborate group were unsatisfactory. The *Geldermalsen* was carrying at least five completed Chinese groups; they must have been from a very expensive and very small special commission, because few examples exist of this Chinese version.

Pl. 203. Glazed polychrome group of 'Tyrolean (or Dutch) Dancers', Meissen, c.1735–7. One of two versions modelled by J.F. Eberlein. 16 cm ht.

Two standing models of crested pheasants, originally decorated in famille rose enamels, were recovered from the *Geldermalsen*, the glazes of both degraded to matt white. Both have the simple outlines, tucked wings and raised head turned sharply backwards that are normally concealed under rich bright pink, green, blue, yellow and turquoise enamels which make these, when in original condition, such dramatic and popular bird figures.[106] The presence on board of these two dates the model firmly to mid-century; though it is, of course, possible that it was made over several decades in small numbers. The bases, moulded as tree stumps, have pierced apertures with ribbing around them meant to simulate knots and holes (Pl. 208). The Chinese painters of bird groups generally coloured the bases naturalistically, in green, aubergine, chocolate-brown or iron-brown, contrasting with the rich plumage. Pheasants derive from parrot models half a century earlier, and, in fact, there was one parrot on the *Geldermalsen*, showing perhaps that these popular models were made later than the normal terminus of c. 1720.[107] The glazes on the parrot, originally bottle green, survived only in tiny indentations within the plumage, but the body is of a distinctive pale brown biscuit, like the group of larger, standing Daoist Immortals whose coloured glazes, too, have entirely disappeared (Pl. 204).

The Dutch bought 'white figures' and 'small figures' sporadically throughout the eighteenth century, and the first must surely have been part of the shipments available at Amoy, the export port for Fujian Province blanc-de-chine at the head of the river along which the kilns lay. Those white wares on the *Geldermalsen* where the glaze has survived in shiny condition, and which had not originally been enamelled, were attributed to Fujian. These included a somewhat coarsely potted group of plump, crouching cranes, the chalky body degraded but showing no vestiges of enamels, whose low quality recalled the non-metropolitan blanc-de-chine lion joss-stick holders on the Asian junk. A large figure of a ferocious Immortal, his attribute unfortunately missing, was set within a rocky grotto and clearly came from Fujian; as was a similar incomplete grotto, without a figure, but applied with prunus branches, and a small demon, both in poor condition.

Most striking among the intact blanc-de-chine figures were two groups of Daoist Immortals, many still retaining their single specific attribute which – in combination with certain facial and clothing details – helped to distinguish one from another (Pls. 201, 205). They were by no means normal export material; the Chinese, for whom they were intended, would have used them on household altars. The rectangular plinth bases were unusually impressed back and front with a small heart-shaped medallion. It is more normal to find such sets of Daoist Immortals, for the Chinese popular market, decorated in opaque rose and other enamels over a coarse brown biscuit body; the bases often have an opaque turquoise glaze. They are traditionally dated 'c. 1800', but this may be too late if they are simply the products of provincial or lower-quality kilns half a century earlier than expected. None of these figures survive in early documentary collections, or are known mounted in eighteenth-century European ormolu.

Other white wares were fragmentary, for the most part. Four small models of recumbent ladies were almost certainly originally brightly coloured (Pl. 205). The

Pl. 204 (opposite page, top). Group of glazed figures from the *Geldermalsen*'s 'private cargo', c.1750. Standing figures 18–20 cm ht, blanc-de-chine standing demon 11 cm ht, seated boy 11.5 cm ht, partially disrobed recumbent lady 14 cm wide.
The group of standing figures are probably all intended as sagacious Daoist Immortals; two at least appear to represent Shoulao with his long beard. The evidence suggests that all were originally covered in a glaze particularly vulnerable to saltwater immersion; the lady, too, was almost certainly brightly enamelled when she left Canton.

Pl. 205 (opposite page, below). Four standing white-glazed figures, and a model of a recumbent lady, c.1750. Standing figures 10 cm ht, lady 13.5 cm long.
The standing figures include the Daoist Immortal Li Tieguai, while the figure with pointed cranium is the stellar god Shoulao (Shouxing), frequently included as a Daoist deity in sets of nine which should in theory only consist of the eight accepted Immortals.

curving bodies, with heads resting against the raised left forearm, may have been ornamental as far as Western buyers were concerned, but were perhaps intended by the Chinese as door handles. Another model, of which only one example was recovered, was specifically decorative; a white-glazed lady reclined comfortably against a small, pierced, drum-shaped table, her legs casually crossed at the ankles, and her simple housecoat unbuttoned to the waist (Pl. 204). Such titillating figures are virtually unknown in export ceramics, although a lady standing *en déshabille* is known in blanc-de-chine. Erotic subjects are more normally found painted rather than moulded on export porcelain; for example, on the underside of vases and bowls. Counterparts to this kind of porcelain figure are found in ivory carvings such as the well-known naked 'medicine ladies', which had rather more of an erotic than a therapeutic content for a Chinese buyer.[109]

Among the 109 human figure models discovered by Hatcher, none were more unexpected or exciting than the ones splashed with simple but bold glazes. They formed a remarkable group of figures, almost certainly made for the domestic Chinese market. They were apparently secular in origin, though it is possible that the two versions of a lady standing with a child derived from more traditional representations of the Bodhisattva Guanyin, Goddess of Mercy, who was on occasion depicted by Chinese potters holding an infant as Patron of Mothers. The elderly dignitary wearing an official hat and raising a boy at his left shoulder has no obvious precedent in earlier models painted with famille verte enamels, from which many of these small mid-century figures probably derived; whereas the blue and white 'piggy-back' group, by contrast, does occur in famille verte (Pl. 208). Many of the figures with clothes in greyish-blue, celadon and clear glazes may originally have had further unfired decoration on top, to judge from a single figure recovered from a later shipwreck. This was a comparable figure of a dignitary, standing on an unglazed low, rectangular base, wearing a long blue-ground coat and white undergarments. It was salvaged from the wreck of the *Middelburg*, a Dutch East Indiaman sunk in 1781 by the English fleet when at anchor in Saldanha Bay, off the Cape Town 'factory' site.[110] Although the figures were cheaper in 1780 than the previous year, when the Heren XVII had initially requested figures to be purchased, the supercargoes' report for 1780 complained that 'some of them are painted with watercolours which dissolve when damp'.[111] This may explain the unsubtle colour washes on most of these glazed figures; the blue, celadon and clear glazes may have been further over-decorated with unfired paints and gilding, to create the sort of elaborately patterned brocaded robes found on more spectacular famille rose figures for which these were an inexpensive alternative.

It is possible, but very unlikely, that the small models of saddled standing horses, and seated boys each holding a peach, would have been enriched in this way. Examples of blue and white seated smiling boys, of the type Hatcher found, survive unblemished in other collections, and clearly never bore further decoration. Earlier versions of these boys were decorated in famille verte enamels[112] and one example was even copied at Meissen, but by mid-century plain blue and white ones are the type most commonly found (Pl. 207). The Chinese have long enjoyed reproducing laughing, happy, well-fed children on porcelain; late Ming blue and white vessels and dishes frequently depict children enthusiastically playing with toys, while some of the finest Qing enamelled wares show mothers or lady attendants adoringly supervising their offspring or charges in tranquil family groups.

There are, however, no obvious antecedents for the small models of saddled but riderless horses, designed – in pairs – with heads turned to look to the left and right (Pl. 206). Famille verte examples exist depicting horses with riders or recumbent;[113] but this discovery of quite a few standing saddled pairs suggests that they

Pl. 206. Group of blue, celadon and white-glazed standing dignitaries and ladies, and a pair of saddled ponies, c.1750. Figures (left to right) 16, 18.5 and 16.5 cm ht, ponies 9.3 cm wide.

Pl. 207. Five small blue-robed boys seated holding up a peach, c.1750. 11.5 cm ht.

Pl. 208. Three exceptionally rare figures from the *Geldermalsen*'s 'private cargo', c.1750. Dignitary 18.3 cm ht, pheasant 26.3 cm ht, 'piggy-back' group 19.8 cm ht.

were either the result of a single special commission, or that, initially, perhaps they were intended for a particular domestic Chinese purpose.

Of all these 'private trade' figures, none were rarer and more fascinated collectors than the two standing ladies wearing simple long robes boldly splashed in a rich copper red on a celadon ground (Pl. 208). It is conceivable that the mottling is in fact an accidental effect of a lucky reduction kiln-firing; if this is so, the red splashes are very fortuitously placed. More likely, an extra mineral flux was applied over the unfired celadon ground, and when fired together this splendid effect was obtained. Figures of this kind are not recorded in any early Western inventory. Had they been available in Europe, surely the great Parisian *marchand-merciers* would have seen the decorative potential of mounting these with ormolu, as exotic rich accoutrements for a grand salon. They are one of the most exciting and novel discoveries in a very remarkable cargo, a cargo which eventually arrived home two centuries late.

We may regret that much was lost during the actual sinking, and that information which might under ideal diving conditions have been recovered could not be recorded as the divers struggled on the murky sea bed. But the cargo of the *Geldermalsen* has afforded pleasure to millions who have now acquired an appreciation of Chinese ceramics, and have a greater knowledge of the rich European society for which the *Geldermalsen*'s cargo was intended. This is perhaps the most pleasing legacy of a very remarkable salvage operation, a moment when art historians, collectors of ceramics, antique dealers and the general public came together to share the excitement of a unique art world occasion.

DISPERSING THE PORCELAIN CARGOES

At the peak of the Western demand for imported Chinese porcelain, over a million pieces a year were flooding into Company warehouses in London, Amsterdam, Copenhagen and Gothenburg. Every Western maritime capital wanted to share in the bonanza of successful Far Eastern trade. Even in bad years, for the Dutch

Chambers forming the VOC gross profits on a cargo were rarely less than 50 per cent on a voyage which they had financed, and over the period 1729–94 they averaged 85 per cent.[114] But there was apparently a certain difficulty in over-supply of Company porcelain on a year-to-year basis as demand became more specific, and particular patterns were asked for which were subsequently delivered in too great a quantity. The Companies were never quite sure what they would end up with, and what they would be able to offer for sale when the ships finally arrived home. One way to anticipate the quantity and quality of porcelain purchases in Canton was to send boxes of samples back with a supercargo; these 'musters' gave an idea of what was stacked in the hold, and the information was supplemented by studying the freight lists drawn up at Whampoa.[115]

Once the pots arrived safely (although breakage was always a source of complaint), the Companies had to sell these vast consignments. In England, this was done through Company auctions organized in the 'General Court Room' of the India House in London; the same auction procedure was used for teas, spices and other imported commodities (Pl. 209). The system was similar in the rest of Europe, as far as published records indicate; no Company had its own retail establishments. In Holland, when the market was buoyant, an individual Chamber would auction its own imports locally; otherwise they could go to Amsterdam auctions.[116] Public auctions offered the considerable advantage that appropriate government and Company import duties could be levied on the auction 'hammer' prices. Even 'private trade' goods could be offered, so that there could be no argument about a fair valuation of the personal imports. These duties were surprisingly high in Britain on imported porcelain and pottery, to protect the native coarse pottery industry;[117] but, until the English Company discontinued any importation of Chinese export porcelain in 1791, the auctions continued to disperse it (despite the duty) more or less successfully.

The essential feature of these huge auctions was that they were primarily wholesale operations. 'Chinamen' buyers recur there regularly over the years, buying in huge quantities, either for the domestic market to make up services and table settings as required by their retail clients or for the huge re-export market; this was particularly true of London 'Chinamen'.[118] The cataloguing was often a little casual. In late 1722, single lots included '1,053 blue and white boats [for sauce], 5 sorts'; '4,970 blue and white sneakers [small drinking cups], more or less in 12 lots, to be taken as they rise from the pile'.[119] 'Private trade' purchases imported for personal profit or use usually – but not always – had to go through the auctions as well, to establish a value; although it was also possible to pay the Company a straight percentage of the value on collection. No doubt a considerable quantity of goods disappeared as ships approached the home wharves of the various European companies. William Hickey records the totally casual way in which a smuggler contracted for a large quantity of tea, both Company cargo and 'private trade', as the ship bearing the diarist home from the East sailed down the international section of the English Channel, where Customs officers could not touch the transaction.

The men and ladies at the public auctions who bought 'as they rise from the pile' were called 'Chinamen'. They advertised their retail china shops in London with elaborate trade cards, boasting the fashion and variety offered at such chic establishments as the 'Three Cannisters', the 'Golden Tea Kettle' or the 'Two Jars' in Holborn.[120] These shops, often doubling as 'India shops', offered a range of exotic imports, as well as expensive, locally manufactured ones. One group was based at the New Exchange in the Strand, and, not surprisingly, others were located in the City of London near the Company warehouses.[121] In the eighteenth century, the principal warehouses storing imported commodities awaiting auction

were in Leadenhall Street, right beside the Company headquarters, though the expensive pepper stocks were held in cellars under the Royal Exchange (Pl. 210). Peter Motteaux had his shop at the 'Sign of the Two Fans', near the Old East India House, a few decades before the *Geldermalsen*'s voyages, where he sold 'China and Japan Wares, Tea, Fans, etc'; the origin was almost immaterial in the public mind, so long as the goods offered were oriental.[122] Porcelain was an important element in the retail 'Chinaman' or 'India shop' business, but there was often a wide range of more luxurious purchases to be made in a good one. At a fashionable establishment, a purchaser could choose silks or lace, have teas blended or buy some chocolate for drinking, select a dinner service, refurbish wallpaper *à la Chinoise*, choose a nest of lacquer tea tables and a new fan, or replace household wine glasses with a bright new set. Many of the wholesaler buyers shipped their bulk purchases around the country, hiring a hall or a shop for a temporary exhibition in the provinces. But, by the 1770s, it was a novelty for would-be purchasers to attend sales themselves in the newly fashionable West End (Pl. 212). From 1766, James Christie had popularized the pleasure for a member of society furnishing an elegant house of buying all manner of goods and art objects at his auctions. At his new Pall Mall auction room, the rich and famous could find in the early catalogues everything from finest soft furnishings and porcelain through to loads of meadow hay, a coffin or a case of Batavian arrack (Pl. 211). After about 1770, being still primarily based in the City, 'Chinamen' did not apparently have such influence on taste by virtue of their 'India house' sale purchases. English ceramics had become sufficiently cheap, desirable and available to fill the front window of a china shop in the increasingly popular West End of mid-Georgian London. Favourable export duties meant that entrepreneurs like Wedgwood and Bentley, with the same new cheap, but fine, British ceramics, were rapidly making great inroads into the markets for both Chinese and native ceramics in Continental Europe; and there was no significant competition from

any locally potted vessels to British exports to the American Colonies.[123] The great decades of the London 'Chinamen' as purveyors of a whole range of imported luxuries seem thus to have been in the second and third quarters of the eighteenth century, and their decline is directly linked to the boom in English ceramics after about 1770.[124] Many big domestic British ceramic factories now had elegant London showrooms, where purchasers could come to examine samples in current taste, and commission services to be painted with their own coat-of-arms or device relatively cheaply. Factory agents and independent merchants could for the first time offer a speedy service which was mercilessly competitive to the ceramic imports of the East India Company, and the picture was little different across Europe. Chinese export porcelain of 'Nanking' type was not to retain its commercial edge in Europe for very long after the ill-fated voyage of the *Geldermalsen*.

Pl. 212. View across two centuries: porcelain from the *Geldermalsen* awaiting auction in Christie's Amsterdam warehouse.

APPENDIX A

The Hatcher Junk Cargo:
Checklist of Shapes and Sizes
of Porcelain Sold at the
Four Christie's Amsterdam Sales

Summary

Cups	8,015
Dishes	2,230
Bowls	5,711
Ewers	1,158
Jars	810
Covered boxes	1,812
Vases	2,186
Other shapes	256
	22,178 pieces

Cups

	6.8 cm diam	6-7.5 cm ht	158 pieces
Stem cups		4.5-5	635
	?	?	577
			1,370
Upright	7	7	9
	7.2	6.5	21
	5	4.3	2,409
	4.7	4	177
			2,616
Shallow	8-8.3		129
	6-7.2		2,582
	4-4.5		28
			2,739
Conical	6.5-6.7		22
Nest of six cups	4.5 to 8		12
Nest of four cups (incomplete?)	5.3 to 7.5		4
Nose drinking cups	10	5	2
	?	?	10
			12
Blue-washed stem cups	6.5	7.2-7.5	289
Yellow-glazed, *lingzhi* handles	7		2
Dehua white-glazed stem cups		6.5-6.6	3
Dehua surprise cups with figure	7.5		29
Dehua half-lychee-shaped cup	8.5		1
			33
Miscellaneous			916
TOTAL			8,015 pieces

Dishes

Kraak ware with flattened rim	47-47.5 cm diam	41 pieces
	34.5-35.5	238
	28.8-30	461
	26-27.5	419
	20-21	303
	14-14.5	17
Kraak saucer-dishes	13.9-14.1	2
		1,481
Non-Kraak, various shapes	19.5-20	12
	17	1
	14-14.5	11
	8.5-11	327
	5.5-7.5	213
	?	35
		599
Octagonal	10.8-11	11
Blue-washed, incised	29.5	2
	19.5-20	30
	?	10
		42
White-glazed, moulding	11.5	54
Brown-glazed, white slip	34-35	6
Celadon-glazed, incised	35-37.5	21
	30-31.5	16
		37
TOTAL		2,230 pieces

Bowls

Kraak ware	34-37 cm diam		44 pieces
	25		1
	13.5-14	7.5 cm ht	71
	11.5-12	6-6.5	9
Klapmutsen	27-27.5		73
	10		103
High, with cover	14	16.5	3
			304
Non-Kraak, various shapes	20-22.5		116
	16-18		435
	12-15		169
	8.5-11.5		2,614
	7.5-8.5		40
	?		138
			3,512
Octagonal	11-12		274
	8.5-9		133
			407
Reticulated	10.5-11.5		46
	9		513
	?		36
Reticulated, octagonal	11-11.5		18
	?		12
			625
With blind fret carving	14.5		30
	13		4
			34
With carved flower heads	21.5		4
	18-18.5		6
			10
Bulb bowls	16		2
With everted flattened rim	20.7		4
Covered	10.5-12		3
	7-8.5		25
Covered, with pierced liner	8		2
Covered, octagonal	8.5		1
	?		144
			175

Lotus-bud-shaped, with three small feet	10-11	5.5-6 ht	20
	8	4	2
	?	?	2
			24
Blue-glazed, incised	21		13
	18.5		19
Blue-glazed, interior white	9		27
	?		51
			110
With underglaze red	9-9.2		19
Covered, with blue and brown decoration, crackle-glazed	15.5		1
White-glazed, octagonal	9		6
White-glazed, octagonal, some incised	?		54
White-glazed, nest of five	8.5-13.5		10
	?		221
White-glazed, moulded as flower heads	14.5		139
White-glazed, ribbed sides	13		9
			439
Celadon, shallow	13		4
Celadon, shallow, ribbed sides	13		6
Celadon, shallow, ribbed sides, incised	13		31
			41
Brinjal, incised, aubergine and pale green washes on soft yellow ground, crackle-glazed	19.5		4
TOTAL			5,711 pieces

Ewers

Kendis

Kraak, bulbous spout, moulded	22.5-24 cm ht	17	pieces
Kraak, bulbous spout, not moulded	20-23	142	
	13.5	285	
Kraak, disc-shaped spout and neck	20.5-23	89	
Transitional, disc-shaped spout and neck	20	11	
Olive-green glaze, bulbous spout	12.5	1	
		545	

Bottles

Kraak, pear-shaped, with long straight neck, moulded	26-27	173
Kraak, pear-shaped, with onion top, moulded	27	113
Transitional, pear-shaped, with long straight neck	23-24	3
	20	18
	?	4
Transitional, double-gourd-shaped	24	2
	19.5-20.5	17
	?	3
Dark-green-glazed, pear-shaped	15	1
Brown-glazed, pear-shaped	15	1
Blue-glazed	?	16
		351

Jugs

Transitional, pear-shaped, with handle but no spout	21.5	2

Tea or wine pots with handle, spout and cover

Globular, upright handle	24-27	19
	15	1
Globular, upright handle, octagonal foot	24-26	11
Globular, loop handle, tapering spout	11.5-14	97
	10.3-10.7	43
Globular, short neck	13.5-14	1
Globular, compressed, short neck and foot rim	14	1
	9-11.5	24

Globular, squared handle	13	1	Transitional, barrel-shaped, slightly domed cover	26-31	141	
				20-21	5	
Globular, miniature	7-7.5	4				
Barrel-shaped, loop handle, S-shaped spout	17-20	4	Barrel-shaped, as above, but slightly waisted	20.5	1	
Oval, loop handle, S-shaped spout, moulded panels	16	2	Barrel-shaped, as above, with carved flower heads	19.5	1	
	9.5	2		9.5-10	11	
Peach-shaped, lotus-bud mouth	18	2		?	2	
						161
Cadogan	15	10	Ovoid, waisted neck, knobbed cover	33	1	
Hexagonal	12-12.3	5				
Blue-glazed, globular	?	6	Ovoid, narrow unglazed neck, drum-shaped cover	28-32	43	
Brown-glazed, short spout, three handles below rim	7.5	2		18-23	155	
				11	1	
				?	30	
Dehua, white-glazed, cylindrical, animal handle and spout	15	2				230
	7.5	6	Compressed globular, slightly domed cover fitted with metal knob and handles	21-22	2	
Dehua, white-glazed, globular, short neck	9-11	12		18.5	3	
				?	1	
		255				6
Miscellaneous	?	5				
TOTAL		1,158 pieces	Jarlets, ovoid, narrow neck with everted rim	9-9.7		21
			Miniature, octagonal baluster with cover	8.5-9		5
			Miniature, various shapes	4.5-6		162
						167

Jars

Guan, knobbed cover	47-49 cm ht	7 pieces	*Guan,* blue and brown decoration, crackle-glazed	15.5		1
	32	2				
	21.5-25.5	52	Stoneware jar, baluster	13.5		1
	?	9	'Jar and cover'	?		4
		70	TOTAL			810 pieces
Lobed, rounded sides	12-12.5	3				
Transitional, baluster, octagonal, knobbed cover	34-36.5	141				
Transitional, baluster, high neck, knobbed cover	31.5-33	4				
	27	1				
		146				

Covered Boxes

Betel boxes, rectangular, rounded sides, notched corners	13-13.5 cm l	19 pieces
Betel boxes, oval, rounded sides	13.5-14	11
		30
Compressed globular	18.5-23 diam	17
	11-11.5	4
Compressed globular, octagonal	20	6
		27
Seal paste, compressed globular, some with pierced liners	8-9.5	87
Cosmetic, compressed globular	5-6	269
Medicine, compressed globular	4.5-6	18
Pill boxes, compressed globular	3.5-5	694
Cylindrical, with flat cover	4.7-5	22
Egg-shaped	6 ht	2
Square	5.5 w	1
Rectangular	7.2 l, 5 w	1
Blue-washed pill boxes, compressed globular	5 diam	555
Green-glazed, domed cover, archaic characters in relief	5-6	2
Celadon-glazed, circular	9.5	3
White-glazed, circular, ribbed sides, impressed medallion on cover	13.5	1
Miscellaneous		100
TOTAL		1,812 pieces

Vases

Rolwagens

Cylindrical, narrow waisted neck and trumpet mouth	47.5-50 cm ht	5 pieces
Cylindrical, short wide neck and rolled rim	44-47	6
	21-23	74
	?	10
		95

Gu beaker vases

	32	4
	21.5-24	60
	?	8
		72

Bottle vases

Globular, tall onion-topped neck	36.5-39	7
Globular, tall neck and flared rim	36.8	1
Globular, tall beaded neck	35-36	2
Globular	35-37.5	9
Mallet-shaped, tall onion-topped neck	37-38	5
Mallet-shaped, tall beaded neck	38.5	1
?	35-39.5	15
		40

Wall vases

Flat-backed, globular, onion-topped neck, animal spout	17.5-18.7	4
Flat-backed, waisted, flaring neck	11.7	2
	?	4
		10

Miniature vases

Various shapes	10-13	1,436
	5.5-8	406
	?	116
		1,958

Other vases

Blue-washed, globular, tall neck and flared rim	13	2
Blue-washed, as above, incised	11.5	2
Dehua, white-glazed, *gu* beaker	21	3
Dehua, white-glazed	16	1
Miscellaneous		3
		11
TOTAL		2,186 pieces

Other Shapes

Incense burners
Bombe sides, slightly
everted rim

22 cm diam		1 piece
20.5		1
12.3		1
10.5		1

Tripod, low cylindrical   11   1

Dehua, white-glazed,
cylindrical, three *ruyi* feet,
impressed and raised
bands

11.3	18.5 ht	1
11.5	8.5	1
8.2	6.5	1
8.5	6	1

Apple-green-glazed,
globular, flaring rim, two
mythical beast loop
handles   12.5   1

                                        10

Brush pots

Cylindrical	20 diam	21.5 ht	1

Cylindrical, incised
design   19.5   19.5   1
                          15-18   10
Cylindrical, concave,
carved and incised designs   21   1

                                        13
Drinking beakers   18 ht   2

Mustard pots
Globular, with handle and
knobbed cover   11-12.5 ht   4

Pear-shaped, with handle
and knobbed cover   11   2

Ribbed, with handle and
knobbed cover   11-11.5   4

                                        10

Garden seat
Barrel-shaped   40.5 ht   1

Cat nightlight
Moulded, pierced,
detachable base   14 ht   13 w   4

Urinal
Globular, cup-shaped,
angled mouth, animal
overhead handle   20 ht   5

Bird-feeder
Compressed globular,
double ring fitting   4-6.5 diam   12

Blue-washed   7   1

                                        13

Zhadou
Flaring mouth   7-7.5 ht   9.5-11 diam   7

Brush-washer
Globular, recessed
mouth   8 diam   2

Trays
Rectangular, notched
corners, blue-washed
interior   14 l   7

Oval   9   20

                                        27

Cricket cages or potpourris
Hexagonal, pierced,
yellow- and green-washed
on the biscuit   9 ht   3

Water droppers
Reticulated peach and
half-peach shape, dark-
green-glazed   12 l   1

Dehua, white-glazed,
moulded as a boy   11 ht   1

Dehua, white-glazed,
moulded as a dignitary   9.5   1

                                        2

Joss-stick holders
Dehua, white-glazed,
moulded as Dogs of Fo   21 ht   23

Figures
Dehua, white-glazed,
moulded as seated
dignitaries   15 ht   6

Moulded as Buddhist
lions   9   9

                                        15

Miscellaneous   118

TOTAL   256
                                        pieces

APPENDIX B

A Dutch Order for Porcelain, 1643

This is an extract from *Porcelain and the Dutch East India Company* by Dr T. Volker, a study of the porcelain trade taken from the Company's archives kept at their Asian headquarters in Batavia, the modern Jakarta, between 1602 and 1682. It provides a record of the porcelain orders for the Dutch market placed in 1643 by the VOC with two merchants, Jousit and Tecklim, as well as some interesting comments on the beginnings of tea-drinking in Europe:

A memorial dated Formosa, April 25th, specifies the porcelains contracted for with the Chinese merchant Jousit 'to be delivered fine, curious and neatly painted' within five months to date, as follows: 500 pots for preserves, octagonal and round; 500 small butter-jars; 3,000 butter-cups with covers; 500 full-sized pear flasks and gourd flasks, 1,000 half-sized, 1,500 third-sized, and 2,000 quarter-sized ditto, ½ pear and ½ gourd; 200 large beakers; 500 beakers; 3,000 mustard-pots; 500 chamber pots; 200 large flower-pots; 1,000 small flower-pots with handles; 1,000 full-sized and 1,000 half-sized wine-jugs with spouts and 2,000 pear-shaped ditto; 2,000 large full-sized, 2,000 half-sized, 3,000 third-sized, 3,000 quarter-sized bowls; 8,000 caudle-cups, 10,000 half-sized and 12,000 third-sized caudle cups; 4,000 full-sized, 6,000 half-sized, 8,000 third-sized octagonal cups; 2,000 small cups 'half cut through'; 2,000 small cups 'wholly cut through'; 10,000 tea-cups, 'outside with four flowers'; 10,000 'rose-cups'; 10,000 bell cups; 1,000 nests of six small cups each; 5,000 rummers; 30,000 small brandy-cups; 20,000 bowls after five samples; 1,000 salt-and-pepper cellars; and 25,000 tea-cups after two samples.'

Among this order for 192,400 pieces, several new forms again appear: octagonal pots for preserves, covered butter-cups, flower-pots with handles, pear-shaped, spouted wine-jugs, small cups 'wholly' and 'half cut through', nests of six small cups, and salt-and-pepper cellars.

The habit of drinking tea was now forming in Europe, where it was started by the Dutch, who had heard about tea for the first time from Van Linschoten's *Itinerario* in 1596. In 1607 they carried tea from Macao to Bantam, the first recorded shipment of tea by any Europeans stationed in East Asia. The first recorded shipment to Europe was in 1610, when the Company bought tea in Hirado and shipped it home via Bantam. Occasional shipments will have reached Holland from this year onward, and on January 2, 1637 the Directors wrote to Batavia: 'As tea begins to come into use by some of the people, we expect some jars of Chinese as well as Japanese tea with every ship.' As a result of this tea-cups were now in stronger demand. Though a few times before this they appear in the bills of lading, they were till now only an Asian trade name for a special kind of small cup not used in Europe for tea. In this year 25,000 are ordered. After this year tea-cups form a more or less constant item in the Company's porcelain trade. From Holland the habit of drinking tea spread to France, Germany and England, where the Dutch imported the new commodity. In England it appeared for the first time in 1650 and in 1660 it was poured in London's coffee-houses, witness Pepys, who wrote in his diary on September 25th of that year: 'I did send for a cup of tee, a China drink, of which I had never drunk before.' It had come to stay, and so had tea-cups, and after a while other tea things, such as pots, saucers, jugs and basins.

Another memorial of the same date specifies the porcelains contracted for with the Chinese merchant Tecklim. It is for: 1,500 large, 4,000 half, 6,000 third and 8,000 quarter-sized dishes; 500 large, 1,000 half, 4,000 third, 12,000 quarter-sized fruit-dishes, the last of three kinds, and 20,000 eighth-sized of four kinds; 4,000 full, 6,000 half, 8,000 third, and 10,000 quarter-sized *clapmutsen*; 12,000 plates with milled rims; 12,000 plates, somewhat more concave; 12,000 dinner plates with flat rims; 5,000 small 'net' dishes; 5,000 *mosschaeltiens* (small vegetable-dishes), and 15,000 small saucers in three kinds.

Among this total of 146,000, new shapes again appear: plates with milled rims and 'concave' plates.

APPENDIX C

Checklist of Dated Ming Transitional Wares, 1625-43

(For book references not given in full, see Bibliography)

1 1625 Large incense burner. 27 cm diam.
Eight Immortals and Shoulao in a landscape.
Dedicatory inscription dated 'Tianqi *yichou*' year.
Illustrated: Little, Fig. 3, p.5.
British Museum (on loan).

2 1625 Incense burner. 17 cm diam.
Scene from 'Romance of the Three Kingdoms'.
Inscribed '5th year Tianqi'.
See Pl. 56.
British Museum.

3 1626 Incense burner. 14 cm diam, 9 cm ht.
Figures in landscape.
Inscribed 'Auspicious day in the *bingyin* year in the
reign of Tianqi of the Ming'.
Illustrated: Kilburn, No. 56, p.108.
Private collection.

4 1634 *Rolwagen*. 45.7 cm ht.
Rocks, bamboo and peonies. Incised borders.
Poem and cyclical date, *jiaxu* year.
Illustrated: Lion-Goldschmidt, Daisy, *Ming Porcelain*,
Pl. 247; Little, Fig. 8, p.8.
Musée Guimet.

5 1634 *Rolwagen*. 43 cm ht.
Phoenix, rocks and flowering plants. Incised borders.
Same poem and cyclical date as 4 above.
Illustrated: Kilburn, Fig. 16, p.33.
Sold Sotheby's, London, 27 June 1974, Lot 92, and
12 May 1976, Lot 101.

6 1636 Brush pot. 23.5 cm ht.
Scene of a drinking party on two moored sampans in a
lake landscape.
Incised cyclical date, *bingzi* year.
Illustrated: Marchant & Son, *Exhibition of Chinese
Blue and White – Wan Li to K'ang Hsi*, London, 1980,
Pl. 10 and covers. Also Kilburn, pp.34, 87, and Little,
pp.66, 67.
Private collection.

7 1636 Small vase. 16.5 cm ht.
Garden scene.
Inscribed 'Written by Yunluize in the summer of the
bingzi year'.
See Pl. 58.
British Museum.

8 1637 Brush pot. 20.3 cm ht.
Figures in landscape. Incised border.
Cyclical date, *dingchou* year.
Illustrated: Ye Peilan, *Gugong Bowuyuan Yuankan*, 1982,
No. 4, pp.47-8, 96, Pl.5 (there dated 1697).
Palace Museum, Beijing.
Brian McElney.

9 1637 *Rolwagen*. 43 cm ht.
Ladies in garden scene. Incised borders.
Cyclical date, *dingchou* year.
Illustrated: Kilburn, No. 60, pp.88, 110.
Private collection.

10 1638 *Rolwagen*. 46.3 cm ht.
Figures in landscape. Incised border.
Cyclical date, *wuyin* year.
Illustrated: Ye Peilan, see 8 above (there dated 1698).
Palace Museum, Beijing.

11 1638 *Rolwagen*. 45 cm ht.
Ladies in a garden. Incised borders.
Cyclical date, *wuyin* year.
Illustrated: Kilburn, Fig. 17, p.34.
Sold Sotheby's, London, 19 April 1967, Lot 91.

12 1638 *Rolwagen*. 31 cm ht.
Figure in landscape. Green wash over the glaze.
Cyclical date, *wuyin* year.
Illustrated: Kilburn, No. 61, pp.110, 193.
Richard de la Mare.

13 1638 Vase in the shape of a funerary urn. 46 cm ht.
Cyclical date, *wuyin* year.
Lady and playing boys in a garden, pomegranate
medallions round the bulbous central section, plantain
leaves below.
See Pl. 57.
British Museum.

14 1639 *Rolwagen*. 48 cm ht.
Mountain landscape.
Cyclical date, *jimao* year.
British Museum (on loan).

15 1639 *Gu* beaker vase. 47 cm ht.
Figures in landscape above; central band of lotus panels
and symbols, pendant leaves below.
Cyclical date, *jimao* year.
Illustrated: Ashmolean Museum, *Eastern Ceramics and
other works of art from the collection of Gerald Reitlinger*,
No. 73 (there dated 1699).
Ashmolean Museum, Oxford.

16 1639 *Gu* beaker vase. 44.8 cm ht.
Vases and fish bowl above, central band of leaf scrolls,
pendant leaves below.
Cyclical date, *jimao* year.
Illustrated: Little, Fig. 10, p.10; Kilburn, Fig. 18, p.34.
Brian McElney.

17 1639 Pure water bowl.
Figures in landscape.
Dedicatory inscription dated to 'twelfth year of
Chongzhen'.
Illustrated: Krahl, Regina, 'A Dated Chinese Porcelain
Bowl of the Transitional Period', *Oriental Art*, Spring
1986, pp.51-3.
Palace Museum, Beijing.

18   1639   Vase.
             Described as 'with tulip decoration'.
             'Cyclical date referring to 1639 or 1699'.
             Jenyns, R. Soame, *Later Chinese Porcelain*, p.18.
             'At Chantilly'.

19   1640   *Gu* beaker vase. 47 cm ht.
             Bamboo, peonies, bird and rocks above, central band
             of 'floating' flower sprays, pendant leaves below.
             Cyclical date, *gengchen* year.
             Illustrated: Kilburn, No. 65, pp.89, 112.
             Dr Philip Mao.

20   1640   Jar. 16.5 cm ht.
             Landscape scroll, table and rocks.
             Cyclical date, *gengchen* year.
             See Pl. 59.
             Sold Christie's, London, February 1979, Lot 52.

21   1640   *Rolwagen*. 45 cm ht.
             Landscapes in fan-shaped and square cartouches.
             With 'floating' flowers and *ruyi* border at neck.
             Cyclical date, *gengchen* year.
             Illustrated: Brown, Claudia, *Chinese Ceramics: The Wong
             Collection,* Phoenix Art Museum, 1982, No. 62.
             Phoenix Art Museum.

22   1641   *Rolwagen*. 40.6 cm ht.
             Figures in landscape.
             Cyclical date, *xinsi* year.
             Illustrated: Little, Fig. 9, p.9. Kilburn, Fig. 19, p.35.
             Ashmolean Museum, Oxford.

23   1643   Covered jar. 26.5 cm ht.
             Scenes from Nature in rectangular cartouches, flowers
             and rocks on cover.
             Cyclical date, *guiwei* year, on cover.
             See Pl. 12.
             Private collection.

24   1643   Cover for jar. 15.5 cm diam.
             Flowering peonies, bamboo and rocks (slightly
             different from 23 above).
             Cyclical date, *guiwei* year.
             See Pl. 13.
             Private collection.

25   1643   Covered mustard pot. 12.7 cm ht.
             Scholar's table and vase.
             Cyclical date, *guiwei* year.
             See Pl. 16.
             Sold Sotheby's, London, May 1971, Lot 222.

APPENDIX D

The Geldermalsen Packing List

The packing list, surviving in a letter to the Zeeland Chamber confirming the purchases taken on board in autumn 1751, is as follows:

171 dinner services *(tafelserviesen)*

63,623 tea cups and saucers *(theegoed)*

19,535 coffee cups and saucers *(koffiegoed)*

9,735 chocolate cups and saucers *(chocoladegoed)*

578 tea pots *(trekpotten)*

548 milk jugs *(melkkommen)*

14,315 flat dinner plates *(tafelborden)*

1,452 soup plates *(soepborden)*

299 cuspidors *(quispedoren)*

606 vomit pots *(spuijgpotjes)*

75 fish bowls *(viskommen)*

447 single dishes *(enkele schalen)*

1,000 nests round dishes *(nest ronde schalen)*

195 butter dishes *(botervlootjes)*

2,563 bowls with saucers *(kommetjes en pieringen)*

821 mugs or English beer tankards *(mugs of Engelse bierkannen)*

25,921 slop bowls *(spoelkommen)*

APPENDIX E

The Geldermalsen Cargo: Checklist of the 'Nanking Cargo' Sale (Christie's Amsterdam, 28 April–2 May 1986)

Although there is inevitably some minor imprecision in the following figures, they have been assembled with the greatest accuracy allowed by the printed records of the auction sale, including the official supplement, and the uncirculated saleroom corrections.

Bowls	No. Sold	Lot Nos.
Batavian Floral pattern, blue and brown, large size (Pl. 191)	562	2501-2528
Batavian Floral pattern, blue and brown, small size	1,923	2529-2577
Batavian Landscape pattern, blue and brown (Pl. 190)	2,527	2578-2635
Bowls and saucer-dishes, Flying Geese pattern, blue (Pl. 192)	1,368 bowls	2636-2701
	1,732 dishes	
Bowls and saucer-dishes, blue and incised	12	2764A
Cape Market, Floral pattern, blue (unglazed centre) (Pl. 193)	1,082	3201-3209 3209A-E
Cape Market, Floral pattern, blue (glazed centre) (Pl. 194)	365	3218-3228
Peony Rock pattern, blue and enamels (Pl. 189)	2,945	3126-3157
Scholar on Bridge pattern, blue, large size	1,919	2702-2764
Scholar on Bridge pattern, blue, small size (Pl. 187)	3,956	3041-3125
Scholar on Bridge pattern, blue and enamels, large size	458	3001-3019
Scholar on Bridge pattern, blue and enamels, middle size	571	3020-3040
Scholar on Bridge pattern, blue and enamels, small size (Pl. 188)	1,388	3168-3188
Two Flying Birds pattern, enamels	118	3158-3160
Butter tubs		
Cylindrical, blue, with arch finial (Pl. 177)	39	4538-4554
Cylindrical, blue and enamels, with arch finial	19	4501-4509
Cylindrical, enamels, with arch finial	27	4566-4575
Cylindrical, blue, with bud finial (Pl. 178)	56	4229-4252
Oval, blue (Pl. 176)	65	4510-4537
Oval, blue and enamels	16	4555-4562
Oval, enamels	32	4563-4565
Cannon	2	1756,1757
Chamberpots		
Various, blue	15	1193-1205 1200A
Cups and saucers		
Chocolate cups and saucers, with handles:		
Chrysanthemum Rock pattern, blue (Pl. 145)	71	5134-5138
Chrysanthemum Rock pattern, blue and enamels (Pl. 146)	1,410	5139-5143

Chrysanthemum Rock pattern, enamels
(Pl. 147)   723   5152-5159
Daisy Terrace pattern,   1,996   396   5160-5172
enamels, with round handles   cups   saucers

Coffee and tea cups and saucers, without handles:
Bamboo and Pine pattern,   1,063   1,013   5716-5733
blue and enamels (Pl. 143)   cups   saucers
Batavian Bamboo and Peony   6,175   [5204-5260
pattern, blue and brown   saucers   [5219A
(Pl. 151)   6,115   [5260A
                                cups
Batavian Fenced Terrace   360   490   5261-5281
pattern, blue and brown   cups   saucers
Batavian Pavilion pattern,   1,554   1,945   5600-5638
blue and brown (Pl. 153)   cups   saucers
Blue Pine pattern, blue,   13,270 10,910 5501-5550
large size (Pl. 140)   cups   saucers
Blue Pine pattern, blue,   4,430   6,207   5551-5597
small size   cups   saucers 5556A
Chrysanthemum Rock pattern,   1,344   1,699   5693-5715
blue and enamels   cups   saucers
Fenced Pine pattern, blue   620   635   5670-5692
and enamels   cups   saucers
Imari Pavilion pattern,   3,960   2,892   5179-5203
blue and enamels (Pl. 142)   cups   saucers 5185A
Pagoda Riverscape pattern,   9,336   10,274 5033-5077
blue, large size (Pl. 137, 141) cups   saucers 5044A
Pagoda Riverscape pattern,   9,318   8,040   5078-5133
blue, small size   cups   saucers 5101A
                                                 5133A

Figure models (animal, bird and human)
(Pl. 200, 201, 204, 205, 206, 207, 208)   101   5734-5766
                                                  5768-5785
                                                  5736A-D
                                                  5742A,B
                                                  5752A,B
                                                  5760A
                                                  5772A
                                                  5784A-D

Flatwares
Dishes, Fish pattern, blue (Pl. 156)   31   1222-1250
Dishes, Fish pattern, blue and enamels
(Pl. 157)   9   1506-1514
Dishes, Fish pattern, enamels (Pl. 158)   4   1501-1505
Dishes and plates, Three Pavilions pattern,   3702-3757
blue and gold (Pl. 174):   3257A-R
  Dishes   326
  Plates   1,578
  Soup plates   690
Dishes and plates, Zigzag Fence pattern,
blue (Pl. 173):   4755-4759
  Dishes   9
  Plates   61
Plates, Boatman and Six-Flower Border
pattern, blue (Pl. 160)   3,789 1673-1755
Plates, Boatman and Six-Flower Border
pattern, blue and enamels   1,218 2001-2028
Plates, Peony and Pomegranate pattern,   3,252 3598-3670
blue (Pl. 134)   3664A
                                                  3670A,B

Plates, Plantain pattern, blue and enamels 2,330 4136-4181
(Pl. 154)   4152A,B
                                                   4180A,B,C
Saucers, flower-moulded, enamels   272   5173-5178
Saucer-dishes, Cape Market, Dragon   526   3229-3241
pattern, blue (Pl. 196)   3241A,B,C
Saucer-dishes, Cape Market, Flower Spray   520   3209C,D,E
pattern, blue (Pl. 195)   3210-3217
Saucer-dishes, Fish pattern, enamels (Pl. 159) 39 3189-3200
Saucer-dishes, Leaping Boy pattern, blue,   668   4576-4616
large size (Pl. 161)   4616A-C
Saucer-dishes, Leaping Boy pattern, blue,
middle size   800   4617-4660
Saucer-dishes, Leaping Boy pattern, blue   820   4661-4694
small size   4694A,B
Soup plates, Empty Sky pattern, blue
(Pl. 163)   58   4131-4135
Soup plates, Willow Terrace pattern, blue
(Pl. 164)   846   4182-4228

Glass bottles, European   53   1057-1092
                                                   1091A-F

Gold, Chinese
'Nanking shoe' ingots   18   1801-1818
Rectangular ingots   107   1819-1925
Irregular fragment   1   1926

Martabans (Pl. 199)   51   5001-5032
                                                   5011A
                                                   5017A-D

Milk jugs (Pl. 183)
Milk jugs, blue, large size   217   4001-4065
Milk jugs, blue, small size   256   4066-4130

Miscellaneous ceramics, Chinese, including private trade   2223-2252
                                                   3158-3167
                                                   3245-3255
                                                   3263-3265
                                                   2242A-C
                                                   2252A
                                                   2253-2256
                                                   3252A-3265I
                                                   5733A

Miscellaneous ceramics, European   56   1001
                                                   1056
                                                   1013A
                                                   1052A,B
                                                   1056A

Miscellaneous ceramics, Japanese   5   3242-3244
                                                   3244A

Miscellaneous metalwork   14   2029-2040

Sauceboats
Brocade border pattern, blue   7   3698-3701
Flowering Shrubs pattern, blue (Pl. 180)   19   3689-3697
Pine and Bamboo pattern, blue (Pl. 181)   69   3671-3688
Pagoda Trellis pattern, blue, oval,
two-handled   4   3701C-D

Service	No. Sold	Lot Nos.
Lattice Fence pattern, blue (Pl. 165):		3501-3597
		3523A-H
Tureens and covers (Pl. 170)	30	
Condiment pots and covers (Pl. 172)	54 pots	
	42 covers	
Salt cellars (Pl. 171)	107	
Dishes, 42 cm diam	27	
Dishes, 39 cm diam	58	
Dishes, 35.5 cm diam	54	
Dishes, 32 cm diam	135	
Dishes, 29 cm diam	111	
Deep dishes, 38 cm diam	30	
Saucer-dishes, 26 cm diam	106	
Plates, 23 cm diam	1,631	
Soup plates, 23 cm diam	559	

Spittoons

Blue (Pl. 184)	80	4695-4726
Blue and enamels	67	4727-4740
Enamels	46	4748-4754
Enamels, with handles	26	4741-4747

Tankards (Pl. 179)

Blue and enamels, large size	15	1571-1581
Blue and enamels, middle size	189	1515-1570
Blue and enamels, small size	470	1582-1672

Tea pots

Bullet-shaped, blue (Pl. 186)	200	2041-2120
Bullet-shaped, enamels	74	2121-2148
Globular, blue (Pl. 185)	46	2149-2170
Globular, blue and enamels	78	2171-2197
Globular, enamels	93	2198-2222
White only	4	5767
Yixing brown stoneware (Pl. 198)	13	3256-3262
		3262A,B

Vomit pots

Blue (Pl. 175)	343	1094-1169
Blue and enamels	46	1170-1192
Enamels	93	1206-1221

Sale sticker for the 'Nanking Cargo' (enlarged).
The lot number was incorporated onto the label on every single piece sold in
the 1986 Christie's auction, making it almost impossible for standard
18th-century export porcelain to be given a false *Geldermalsen* provenance.

FOOTNOTES

Publications not given in full or referred to as op. cit. are listed in the Bibliography.

Chapter I

1 Reischauer, Edwin O., and Fairbank, John K., *East Asia: The Great Tradition,* Boston, 1960, pp.214-17.

2 Needham, J., *Science and Civilisation in China,* Vol.IV:3, Cambridge University Press, 1971, pp.487-94.

3 Viraphol, S., *Tribute and Profit: Sino-Siamese Trade, 1652-1853,* Harvard University Press, 1977, pp.28-41.

4 Needham, op. cit., p.256.

5 Ng Chin-keong, 'The Fukienese Maritime Trade in the Second Half of the Ming Period – Government Policy and Elite Group's Attitudes', *Nanyang University Journal,* Vol.V, 1971, pp.81-9.

6 Needham, op. cit., p.526, note f.

7 *The Book of Duarte Barbosa,* Vol.I, Hakluyt Society, 1908, pp.145-6.

8 Chang Tien-tse, *Sino-Portuguese Trade from 1514 to 1644,* E.J. Brill, Leiden, 1934, p.33.

9 *The Suma Oriental of Tome Pires,* Vol.I, Hakluyt Society, 1944, pp.103-27.

10 Meilink-Roelofsz, M.A.P., *Asian Trade and European Influence in the Indonesian Archipelago between 1500 and about 1630,* Martinus Nijhoff, The Hague, 1962, pp.169-70.

11 Ts'ao Yung-ho, *Chinese Overseas Trade in the Late Ming Period,* International Association of Historians of Asia, Second Biennial Conference Proceeding, Taipei, 1962, pp.431-2.

12 Meilink-Roelofsz, op. cit., pp.245-7.

13 Ibid, pp.237-8 and 262-8.

14 Blussé, Leonard, 'Chinese Trade to Batavia during the Days of the VOC', *Archipel 18,* Paris, 1979, p.19.

15 Ng Chin-keong, *Chinese Trade with Southeast Asia in the 17th and 18th Centuries,* Colloquium on Trade and Shipping in the Malay Archipelago before 1900, University of Malaya, Kuala Lumpur, 1984, pp.18-22.

16 This pair of temple vases are the earliest firmly dated pieces of blue and white. However, the use of underglaze blue is so assured as to suggest that it had been in use for some time before 1351. The vases may be seen at the Percival David Foundation of Chinese Art, 53 Gordon Square, London WC1.

17 Sayer, Geoffrey R., *Ching-te-chen T'ao Lu or the Potteries of China,* London, 1951, pp.29-30.

18 Dillon, pp.84-5.

19 Ibid, pp.107-8, 118.

20 Ibid, pp.29 and 140.

21 Medley, Margaret, 'Ching-te-chen and the Problem of the "Imperial Kilns" ', *SOAS Bulletin,* No.29, 1966, pp.326-38.

22 Dillon, p.29.

23 Medley, op. cit., p.337.

24 Dillon, p.32. The figure for 1577 is from Yuan Tsing, 'The , 'The Porcelain Industry at Ching-te-chen 1550-1700', *Ming Studies,* No.6, 1978, p.47.

25 Yuan, op. cit, p.47.

26 See Chronology for dates.

27 Volker, p.22, note 7.

28 Ibid, pp.23-4 and 50-51.

29 Dillon, p.33.

30 Reischauer and Fairbank, op.cit., p.337; Dillon, p.154.

31 Dillon, pp.149-56.

32 Lin Xin-Yuan and Bai Kun, 'Concerning the Hu-tien Kiln Site', *Wen Wu,* No.11, 1980, translated into English in Tichane, Robert, *Ching-te-chen: Views of a Porcelain City,* New York, 1983. Also Addis, Sir John, 'A Visit to Ching-te-chen', *Transactions of the Oriental Ceramic Society,* Vol.41, London, 1975-7.

33 Volker, p.27.

34 Bushell, Stephen, *Oriental Ceramic Art,* New York, 1899, p.352.

35 Volker, p.23.

36 Dillon, pp.127-9; Cahill, James, ed., *Shadows of Mount Huang: Chinese Painting and Printing of the Anhui School,* exhibition catalogue, University Art Museum, Berkeley, 1981, pp.19-24; Ho Ping-ti, 'The Salt Merchants of Yang-chou: A Study of Commercial Capitalism in Eighteenth Century China', *Harvard Journal of Asian Studies,* 17, 1954, pp.130-68. Dillon and Cahill refer frequently to the following studies in Chinese and Japanese: Fu Yising, *Ming Qing Shidei Shangren Ji Shangye Ziben (Merchants and Mercantile Capital in the Ming and Qing Periods),* Beijing, 1956; Chen Ye, 'Lun Huizhou Shangye Ziben de Xingchen ji qi tese' ('Discussion of the Form and Special Characteristics of Commercial Capitalism in Huizhou'), *Anhui Shixue Tongxun,* Anhui, 1958; Fujii, Hiroshi, 'A Study of the Xinan Merchants', *Toko Gakuho,* Vol.36, Part 1, Tokyo, 1953-4, pp.1-44.

37 Boxer, C.R., *Fidalgos in the Far East,* 1550-1770, Oxford University Press, Hong Kong, 1968, p.6.

38 Wills, John E., Jr., 'Maritime China from Wang Chih to Shih Lang', *From Ming to Ching,* ed. Spence, Jonathan D., and Wills, John E., Jr., Yale University Press, 1979, p.236, note 15. The calculation from Chinese customs revenues is quoted from Chaunu,

Pierre, *Les Philippines et le Pacificique des Ibériques (XVIe, XVIIe and XVIIIe Siècles): Introduction Methodologique et Indices d'Activité,* Paris, 1960, pp.34, 200-205 and 268. For a good summary, see Attwell, William S., 'International Bullion Flows and the Chinese Economy', *Past and Present,* 95, May 1982, pp.68-90.

39 Cahill, op. cit., pp. 19-21.

40 Certainly by the early eighteenth century, private factories had been established on a large scale. Père D'Entrecolles wrote in 1712, 'King-te-chen is estimated to contain 18,000 households, but some of the large merchants have premises of vast extent, lodging a prodigious multitude of workmen, so that the population is said to number over a million souls.' (Bushell, op. cit., p.283). However, the years of political turmoil after 1645 seem likely to have interrupted the expansion of the late Ming factories and those seen by D'Entrecolles may not have developed until shortly before the turn of the century.

41 Marchant; Kilburn; Frits Lugt Collection, exhibited at the Netherlands Institute, Paris, 1981; Ashmolean Museum; Brown, Claudia, *Chinese Ceramics: The Wong Collection,* exhibition catalogue, Phoenix Art Museum, 1982; *Allison Collection,* Asian Art Museum, San Francisco, 1982; *The Silk Road on the Sea,* exhibition catalogue, Kobe City Museum, 1982; Little, *Chinese Ceramics;* Jorg, C.J.A., *De Hatcher Schenking,* exhibition catalogue, Groeninger Museum, 1984; Butler, *Chinese Porcelain.*

42 Van der Pijl-Ketel; and Dumas, *Fortune de Mer a l'Ile Maurice,* Atlas Film S.A., Paris, 1981.

43 Impey, Dr Oliver, *Ceramics,* first issue, 1986, pp.11-12.

44 The Chinese divide the calendar into cycles of sixty years. Each year is given a name in two characters. The date referred to can be determined from a table and by knowing the dates on which the cycles began. Thus the *guiwei* year is the twentieth of the cycle that began in 1624. For a full explanation and table, see Hobson, R.L., *The Wares of the Ming Dynasty,* Tuttle, Tokyo, 1962, pp.186-7.

45 It should be borne in mind that dated inscriptions cannot invariably be taken as having been written on the date stated, although the 1643 date on the Hatcher covers is well supported. For example, a typical late Wanli (1573-1619) censer with heavy pencilled drawing sold at Sotheby's Hong Kong (Edward Chow Collection, part III), 19 May 1981, Lot 422, was inscribed 'Humbly presented in the Yiwei year of the Yongle reign of the Great Ming', equivalent to 1415. A smaller censer with the same shape and decoration sold at Sotheby's Hong Kong, 29 November 1977, Lot 42, had a six-character Wanli mark. The purpose of a retrospectively dated inscription, on a piece which makes no attempt to imitate earlier wares, is difficult to imagine!

46 Donnelly, Pl.74A.

47 Volker, p.50.

48 Ibid, pp.50-51.

49 Ibid, pp.55-6.

50 Ibid, p.53 and note 16.

51 Ibid, p.54.

52 Ibid, p.105.

53 Kilburn, p.14.

54 Jenyns, *Later Chinese Porcelain,* p.26; Kilburn, p.21. See Glossary for a definition of Kraak ware.

55 An order from Thailand in 1637 requests '60 *corgees* (of food-dishes) each in an assortment gradually enlarging as indicated by the accompanying rattan measure'. Volker, p.78. A *corgee* was usually 20 pieces (p.35, note 3).

56 Brankston, who visited Jingdezhen in the 1930s, described how 'the potter, with amazing skill, throws cups and bowls of identical shape and size in quick succession. These he places on a long plank which is then carried to a second man who presses the vessel over a mould of the exact shape required.' Brankston, A.D., *Early Ming Wares of Ching-te-chen,* Henri Vetch, Beijing, 1938, p.65.

57 Volker, pp.23-35, 39 and 40-56.

58 A classification for Kraak wares by their border patterns, with tentative datings for each group, was proposed by Brian McElney in the catalogue of the Oriental Ceramic Society of Hong Kong's 1979 exhibition, *South East Asian and Chinese Trade Pottery,* pp.34-6. More recently, Maura Rinaldi has suggested some amendments to these groups and their dates in the Singapore National Museum publication *Heritage,* No.8, 1986, pp.1-28. This article is an extract from a book on Kraak ware to be published shortly.

59 Bergstrom, J., *Dutch Still-life Painting in the Seventeenth Century,* London, 1956.

60 Volker, p.23.

61 Pope, John Alexander, *Chinese Porcelains from the Ardebil Shrine,* Sotheby, London, 1981, Pl.108. The terminal date of 1607 for pieces entering the Ardebil Collection is given by Basil Gray in 'Chinese Ceramics in the Topkapi Saray Museum, Istanbul', *Oriental Art,* Winter 1986-7, p.411.

62 A number of shards were recovered from the *Witte Leeuw* of types normally dated half a century earlier. It may be that production continued for several decades longer than we have suspected, as was the case with Kraak wares in the seventeenth century, but accepting these pieces as contemporary with the wreck of the *Witte Leeuw* in 1613 certainly involves some adjustment to our current dating of sixteenth-century export wares.
  There are two bowls – 3.21.6 and 15 in the *Witte Leeuw* catalogue – with Jiajing (1522-66) marks. One is written in distinctive 'grass' characters, which appear on many pieces usually accepted as being of the period. The rounded, rather upright bowl shape is also associated with the mid-sixteenth century.
  There are also dishes with a short, curved cavetto and flattened, straight rim – 3.21.8, 11, 13 and 14 – of a type thought to have been superceded early in the Wanli period by the panelled Kraak style as seen on 1.9.2 and 3. Their fine quality, shape, decorative arrangement and precise drawing seem to separate these from the other *Witte Leeuw* dishes. 3.14, 3.21.7 and 12 are coarser pieces in the same style.

To confuse the issue, there *was* a revival of interest in Jiajing styles at about the time the *Witte Leeuw* sank, and the Jiajing mark later began to be used retrospectively, although I know of no marked pieces earlier than the last few years of the Ming (Kilburn, pp.23, 38).

63 Spriggs, *Red Cliff Bowls,* drew attention to one of these bowls with a Tianqi mark and to another in a painting by Jacques Linard dated 1627.

64 There are dishes with 'net' pattern with Tianqi marks in the British Museum and the Tokyo National Museum.

65 Dillon, p.139, quoting from the *Draft History of Jingdezhen (Jingdezhen taoci shigao),* compiled by the Jiangxi Light Industry Bureau, 1959, p.99.

66 A possible exception is the large dish with six-character Tianqi mark in the Nezu Museum, Tokyo, illustrated in Little: *Chinese Ceramics,* Fig.4, p.5.

67 Bushell, op. cit., p.289.

68 It was stated in a treatise written in 1637 that 'three grades of cobalt oxide used in the blue colouring were obtainable in the area; a high-quality pigment from Zhejiang, and less good from Jiangxi and Guangdong'. Dillon, p.93, quoting from the *Tiangong Kaiwu* by Song Yingxing.

69 See Shepherd, Anna O., *Ceramics for the Archaeologist,* Carnegie Institue of Washington, 1957, pp.233-6.

70 For a Shang bronze *gu* beaker vase, see *Bronzes Archaiques Chinois au Musæ Cernuschi,* Vol. 1, Paris, 1977, no.36.
    Gui incense burners with handles following archaic bronze forms (see *Cernuschi,* no.11) were made in porcelain from the sixteenth century. The earliest I know of without handles is the small one in the British Museum dated 1612, illustrated by Garner, Sir Harry, *Oriental Blue and White,* Faber, London, 1970, pl.55B.
    For *zun* and *hu* bronze shapes, compare Watson, William, *Ancient Chinese Bronzes,* Faber, London, 1962, Pl.6b and 7b with Kilburn, Pl.66 and 73. See also Watson, Pl.72, for a *hu* covered jar shape in bronze.

71 Krahl, Regina, 'A Dated Chinese Bowl of the Transitional Period', *Oriental Art,* Summer 1986, pp.51-3.

72 Little: *Chinese Ceramics,* No.42.

73 Marchant, No.28; Kilburn, No.38.

74 Volker, p.37.

75 Ibid, p.77.

76 Spriggs: *Ginger Jars,* pp.95-6. The typical Kangxi 'ginger jar' is actually broader and squatter than the Hatcher ones, with domed rather than drum-shaped covers.

77 Volker, pp.43 and 50.

78 *Witte Leeuw,* types 1.5, 1.6.2, 2.0, 3.9 and 3.19; Marchant, No.32; Kilburn, Nos.27, 54, 55; also on an early Transitional *rolwagen*

(Butler: *Chinese Porcelain,* No.7) and occasionally on later Transitional pieces.

79 These borders appear most frequently on covered boxes, 'ginger jars' and tea pots among the Hatcher wares. The best illustration in this book is on the underside of the dish in Pl.95.

80 Kilburn, p.38 and Nos. 93, 95, and 102. Nos.95 and 100-104 show various forms of 'Master of the Rocks' drawing, which is in fact no more than a linear drawing technique copied from paintings and prints.

81 Medley, Margaret, *Illustrated Catalogue of Porcelains Decorated in Underglaze Blue and Copper Red,* Percival David Foundation, London, 1963, Nos.696 and B618; Marchant, No.20.

82 Kilburn, pp.14, 41-6, 160-61.

83 Cahill, op. cit., p.34.

84 Curtis, pp.161-73. In a lecture entitled 'Reflections on Dating Seventeenth-century Chinese Ceramics' given at the Asian Art Museum, San Francisco in February 1987, Mrs Curtis amplified her comments, particularly with regard to landscape painting as a means of dating seventeenth-century porcelain. It is to be hoped that this interesting lecture will be published in due course.

85 In a letter to the writer.

86 Frank, Ann, *Chinese Blue and White,* Collector's Blue Books, London, 1969, p.70.

87 Tzio Soen-hong, *The Study of Wan-Yiu (History and Ceramic Art),* Association of Research Institute of Literature and History, Monograph No. 2, Chu Hai College, Hong Kong.

88 Donnelly, p.61. See also Freedman, David, *Blanc de Chine,* exhibition catalogue, S. Marchant and Son, London, 1985, and the review of this exhibition by Dr Oliver Impey (see above, note 43.)

89 I am not certain that all these white wares are from the Dehua kilns. Some may be from other Fujian kilns, or from Jingdezhen. The covered boxes could be from Anxi in Fujian, which had produced boxes of this kind since Song times. See Hughes-Stanton, P. and Kerr, Rose, *Kiln Sites of Ancient China,* Oriental Ceramic Society, London, 1980, pp.24 and 128.

90 Krahl, pp.233 and 240.

91 Volker, pp.65, 93, 101, 103 and 106.

92 By David Howard of Heirloom and Howard, who also noted individual pieces ranging from oatmeal to a strong green almost the colour of verdigris.

93 There is a blue-glazed dish with incised dragons in the British Museum which has a Shunzhi mark. See Jenyns: *Later Chinese Porcelain,* Pl.VI.

94 Christie's Amsterdam, sale catalogue, 14 March 1983, Lots 10-15.

95 Kilburn, No.213.

96 A brinjal bowl in the Asian Art Museum, San Francisco has a Tianqi mark (see Little: *Chinese Ceramics,* Pl.43). However, this bowl seems to stand on its own in the Tianqi period, not only for its biscuit glaze, but also in its shape and the writing of the mark, and it is not universally accepted, despite the support of the Hatcher bowls.

97 Kilburn, pp.38-9.

98 Butler, Sir Michael: 'Chinese Porcelain at the End of the Ming' and *Chinese Porcelain: The Transitional Period.*

Chapter II

1 Howard and Ayers, p.17.

2 Davis, R., *The Rise of the English Shipping Industry,* Macmillan, London, 1962, chapter 1.

3 See, for example, Godden, p.21, for the English growth in South Asian waters.

4 See the catalogue of the exhibition, *Bibliotheca Eugeniana, Die Sammlungen des Prinzen Eugen von Savoyen,* Austrian National Library, Vienna, 1986, nos 53 and 54, for a discussion of the origins of the main 'Company Atlas' and the 'Secret Atlas'.

5 Jorg: *Porcelain,* p.17.

6 Jorg: *Geldermalsen,* p.11.

7 Jorg: *Porcelain,* passim.

8 Ibid.

9 *Chinese Ivories from the Shang to the Qing,* exhibition catalogue, Oriental Ceramic Society, 1984, pp.36-43.

10 Ibid, p.62.

11 Jorg: *Geldermalsen,* p.15.

12 Godden, pp.28 and 30.

13 Ibid, p.33.

14 Jorg: *Porcelain,* p.67 et seq.

15 An interesting chronology for these waterfront views has been established by Crossman, pp.259-65.

16 Jorg: *Geldermalsen,* passim.

17 Godden, pp.36 and 38. Note that the English Company was using sago for packing porcelain in 1700 and as late as the 1790s; Jorg: *Porcelain,* p.86, writes that the VOC only bought it in the years 1757-77.

18 Jorg: *Porcelain,* passim.

19 The link between tea wares and the illegal tea trade was discussed by Dr H.Z. Kent in an unpublished paper presented to the Oriental Ceramic Society, London, 1985.

20 Godden, p.34.

21 Tamasin, A., and Glubok, S., *Voyaging to Cathay,* Viking Press, New York, 1986, p.6.

22 See the sale catalogue for the history of this ill-fated ship and its cargo, *The Bredenhof Bullion,* Christie's Amsterdam, 4 December 1986.

23 Jorg: *Porcelain,* p.89. The VOC banned its shipment to Canton as early as 19 July 1750 (see p.342).

24 The archival information on which this chapter draws extensively was almost entirely discovered by Dr Christian Jorg and his assistants, and used by him as the historical core of his book, *The Geldermalsen: History and Porcelain.*

25 Jorg: *Geldermalsen,* p.41.

26 Ibid.

27 Ibid, pp.44-7.

28 Ibid, pp.45-8, passim.

29 Ibid, p.59.

30 Ibid, p.35.

31 Ibid, p.34.

32 Ibid, pp.34-35.

33 Godden, p.128.

34 Ibid, p.15.

35 Detweiler, p.54.

36 This can be well seen in the film footage shot by John Bremer, later used in the BBC film of the recovery expedition and the auction sale.

37 See Howard and Ayers, passim.

38 Clair, p.134.

39 Jorg: *Porcelain,* p.187.

40 Ibid, pp.164-6 and 186-7.

41 Ibid, pp.110, 112, 115, for drawings of different cups required.

42 Ibid, p.188.

43 Ibid.

44 Ibid, pp.186-7.

45 Ibid, pp.165-6.

46 Ibid, p.164.

47 Detweiler, p.30.

48 Ibid, p.31.

49 Ibid, p.53.

50 Jorg: *Porcelain,* p.166.

51 Clunas, C., 'The West Chamber in Porcelain Decoration', *Transactions of the Oriental Ceramic Society,* Vol.46, London, 1983, p.79.

52 Jorg, *Geldermalsen,* p.83.

53 Ibid.

54 An abbreviated copy of the original shipping invoice is published and discussed by Jorg: *Geldermalsen,* p.59.

55 Jorg: *Porcelain,* p.173.

56 Clair, p.133.

57 Ibid, passim.

58 Somers Cocks, A., *Masterpieces of Cutlery and the Art of Eating,* Victoria and Albert Museum, London, 1976, p.19.

59 Bayne-Powell, p.103; Palmer, p.8.

60 Bayne-Powell, p.103.

61 A Frenchman's observation, published in 1719.

62 Detweiler, passim, provides a particularly detailed analysis of these increasingly elaborate services 'in the French manner' by examining George Washington's ceramic purchases.

63 Bayne-Powell, p.78.

64 Ibid.

65 Ibid, p.74.

66 Jorg: *Geldermalsen,* p.61.

67 Ibid.

68 Jorg: *Porcelain,* pp.172-3.

69 Godden, p.128.

70 Clayton, p.364.

71 Ibid, p.447, illustrates several upright silver salts, all dated c.1700.

72 Clark, p.173.

73 Jorg: *Geldermalsen,* p.63.

74 Ibid, p.59.

75 Ibid, p.81.

76 Ibid.

77 Ibid, p.87.

78 Ibid.

79 Ibid, p.93.

80 Ibid.

81 Ibid, p.63.

82 Ibid.

83 Godden, p.135, cites an order specifying this requirement as late as 1777.

84 Clayton, p.324.

85 Jorg: *Geldermalsen,* p.79.

86 Ibid, p.73.

87 Clayton, p.325; an example hallmarked for 1740 is illustrated as a sauce boat.

88 Jorg: *Geldermalsen,* p.73.

89 See Detweiler, p.161, for the Chinese blue and white bottle and basin owned by George Washington, a type which he referred to as 'Wash hand Guglets and Basons'.

90 Godden, p.160.

91 Jorg: *Porcelain,* p.178.

92 The 1764 order is noted by Jorg: *Porcelain,* p.168.

93 Jorg: *Geldermalsen,* p.71.

94 Clayton, p.416, comments on the surprisingly small numbers of silver tea pots extant from the period c.1755-70, and suggests that porcelain ones may have supplanted the metal variety.

95 Quoted by Godden, p.28, from the shipping requirement for the English ship *Sidney* in 1702.

96 Clayton, p.415.

97 Jorg: *Geldermalsen,* p.59, quoting the shipping invoice.

98 Kjellberg, S.V., *Svenska Ostindiska Compagnierna 1731-1831,* Malmö, 1975, p.313.

99 A 'Gotheborg' saucer-dish in an English private collection has a note affixed that it 'was raised in 1878 by the late Mr Chudley, and was purchased at Mr Lawson Tait's sale on 22 February 1893'.

100 As early as 1699, the *Macclesfield* included in its cargo from Canton some 2,000 tea bowls listed as 'buff-coloured, without'.

101 Jorg: *Geldermalsen,* p.95.

102 Ibid.

103 An example is illustrated by Howard and Ayers, no.139.

104 Jorg: *Porcelain,* p.176; an example is illustrated by du Boulay, A., *Christie's Pictorial History of Chinese Ceramics,* Phaidon-Christie's, Oxford, 1984, p.297.

105 Jorg: *Porcelain,* p.175.

106 A comparable example is illustrated by du Boulay, op. cit., p.300.

107 Two famille verte examples are illustrated by du Boulay, op. cit., p.299.

108 Howard and Ayers, p.35.

109 *Chinese Ivories from the Shang to the Qing,* op. cit., p.112.

110 Illustrated in Jorg: *Porcelain,* p.153.

111 Ibid, p.176.

112 See du Boulay, op. cit., p.289, no.11.

113 The closest enamelled prototype seems to be the pair of horses with riders illustrated by du Boulay, op. cit., p.288, no.5.

114 Jorg: *Porcelain,* p.134.

115 Godden, p.46.

116 Lunsingh Scheurleer, p.65.

117 Toppin, p.39.

118 Godden, passim.

119 Ibid, p.125.

120 Toppin, pp.44-50.

121 Ibid, p.46.

122 Ibid, p.48.

123 Detweiler, pp.53-62, documents the growing preference at Washington's Mount Vernon for the products of new English factories.

124 Toppin, p.48.

GLOSSARY

Apple green A translucent emerald green enamel applied over the glaze as a 'self-colour'; in some cases it is applied over a crackled grey glaze.

Armorial Wares decorated with a European coat-of-arms as a special commission for the family bearing that heraldic coat.

Bai dunzi Prepared white China stone, the feldspathic, non-plastic, vitrifying ingredient essential for the manufacture of white porcelain and of the glazes used for this type of ware. Also known as 'petuntse', the term literally means 'little bricks'.

Baluster vase A vase with a cylindrical neck and trumpet mouth, sometimes described as a *yanyan* vase; Qing dynasty and later.

Batavian ware This is a trade name applied to wares of the Kangxi period and later. They have glazes varying from coffee-coloured to old gold, combined with white medallions or ornamental panels, which are decorated either in underglaze blue, or in overglaze enamels. The name owes its origin to the fact that the Dutch carried great quantities of these wares, transhipping them at their trading station at Batavia.

Biscuit (Bisquit) A term applied to ceramic wares that have been fired, but not yet glazed. The temperature of this first firing varies between about 800-1300° C., according to the constituents of the body and the type of glaze to be applied.

Blanc-de-chine *(see Dehua)*

Bottle vase A pear-shaped vase with contracted neck and flaring lip.

Brinjal bowl About 20 cm or less in diameter, with flared or everted rims, these bowls are roughly incised with flower and leaf sprays, in yellow, green and aubergine lead silicate enamels in various combinations, applied directly to the biscuit.

Brocade designs As the name implies, some of these designs derive from textiles. The term is generally associated with flowers, or close floral scrolls in bright colours against a pink, green, yellow or blue enamel ground, sometimes incised with formal scrolling patterns.

Brush pot A flat-based, cylindrical jar for holding writing or paint brushes.

Brush washer This is usually a small, shallow bowl with straight sides, often with a flat base without a foot-ring.

Café-au-lait A lustrous brown glaze, with a wide range of tones, derived from iron. It became especially popular in the eighteenth century.

Celadon A term applied broadly to wares having a greyish or brownish body covered by a transparent or opaque olive or greyish-toned glaze. The name is derived from the shepherd Celadon in the stage version of Honoré D'Urfé's pastoral romance *L'Astrée*, who wore ribbons of a soft grey-green tone.

Chatter marks These are radiating ridges, varying in prominence, on the base of a circular vessel. They are a fault in manufacture which occurs in cutting the foot-ring, and is due to holding the foot-turning tool insufficiently firmly or at the wrong angle.

Chinese Imari An export ware decorated in underglaze blue, overglaze red enamel and gold, in imitation of somewhat similar wares made at Arita in Japan, whence they were carried by the Dutch merchants in the late seventeenth and early eighteenth centuries through the port of Imari in Nagasaki Bay. The decorative motives are part-Japanese and part-Chinese, arranged in confused patterns over the whole surface.

Clobbered China Chinese underglaze blue, and occasionally red, decorated porcelains 'improved' in Europe by the addition of green, yellow, red and other enamels and gilding, often in such a way as to overlap and disfigure the Chinese designs. The practice began in the eighteenth century.

Compagnie des Indes Chinese porcelains made specifically to European order, and sometimes design, gained this name in the late seventeenth century, when East India Companies other than the Dutch began to take a large share in the Chinese trade.

Crackle This is a phenomenon caused by the unequal contraction of body and glaze during cooling in the kiln, resulting in a crazy paving effect. Technically a fault, it was exploited by the Chinese from the middle of the twelfth century onward for its decorative effect.

Dehua A superlatively fine white porcelain with clear glaze produced at Dehua in the province of Fujian. It varies in tone from a cold, almost grey, white to a warm creamy colour. Although bowls, dishes and vases were produced, it is the figures that are best known in the West. An alternative name for the ware, introduced in France in the nineteenth century, is blanc-de-chine.

Dog of Fo A Buddhist guardian lion, which from the fifteenth century onward occurs as a ceramic decoration and later as a statuette. It is a creature somewhat resembling a Pekinese dog, with a large bushy tail, often shown playing with a brocaded ball decorated with ribbons.

Doucai 'Opposed colours' or 'contrasted colours', a term for porcelains of the Ming and Qing dynasties decorated in a particularly refined and delicate style. The underglaze blue outline to the main parts of the design are filled in with overglaze translucent enamels in a fairly wide range of colours and tones.

'Egg and spinach' Green, yellow and white lead silicate enamel glazes that occur together on the same piece, but not in an organized pattern. This type of decoration first occured under this name during the Kangxi period as a variant of 'tiger skin'.

Eggshell An extremely thin, pure white porcelain, sometimes with a ruby enamel back.

Eight Buddhist Emblems Also known as 'Happy Omens', these often appear on the later ceramic wares, lacquers and cloisonné. The emblems are the Chakra or Wheel, the Conch Shell, the Umbrella, the Canopy, the Lotus, the Vase, the Paired Fish, and the Entrails, or Endless Knot. A bell is occasionally substituted for the Chakra. At times some of these emblems may be mixed up with some of the Eight Daoist Emblems.

Eight Daoist Immortals   These were persons who, for various reasons, achieved immortality. Three were historical figures and the rest were purely legendary.

Eight Daoist Emblems   The attributes of the Eight Immortals.

Eight Precious Things   These often occur as decorative motives and occasionally individually as marks. They are the Jewel; the Cash, a circle enclosing a square; the Open Lozenge, with ribbons; the Solid Lozenge, also with ribbons; the Musical Stone, a roughly L-shaped object suspended from the angle; the Pair of Books; the Pair of Horns; and the Artemisia Leaf. The last is particularly common as a ceramic mark, especially in the Kangxi period.

Enamel on biscuit   This is the application of soft lead silicate enamels to a vessel that has previously been fired without any glaze on it. This initial firing is often to the temperature required for porcelain, i.e. to about 1,250°C. or above; after the application of the enamels, the piece was fired again at a somewhat lower temperature.

Entrepot   A trading centre where products from different countries were exchanged by barter, wholesale or retail trading.

'Factory'   The early name for the building established by a Western trading company abroad to control its local purchasing and selling of merchandise. The individual merchants based there were known as 'factors'.

Famille jaune   A group of enamel-decorated porcelains of the Kangxi period and later, in which the predominant colour is yellow. The group was distinguished by Jacquemart in the nineteenth century.

Famille rose   A term coined by Jacquemart in the nineteenth century and applied to a group of overglaze-enamelled porcelains which begin about 1721. The delicate rose pink which is characteristic of the group is an opaque colour derived from colloidal gold. All the colours in the group are opaque and stand up more in relief than those of the famille verte translucent type.

Famille verte   Another term coined by Jacquemart in the nineteenth century, it applies to a group of translucent enamelled wares on which the predominant colour is green. One colour, iron-red, was opaque, but this rarely plays an important part in the decoration. The use of green enamel has its origin in pieces made as early as the thirteenth century, but the term 'famille verte' is applied only to types made from the seventeenth century onward, which differ greatly in style from earlier wares.

Famille noire, a dull black ground covered with a green enamel, is a variant of famille verte.

Flaming pearl   A motive usually found in association with dragons, occurring in most types of ceramics.

Gao ling   A white firing, plastic china clay first discovered and used by the Chinese potters. Also known as 'kaolin', the term means 'high ridge', named after the area where it is found.

Garniture de cheminée   A set of five pieces for arrangement on a mantelpiece. Three pieces are covered jars, one of which is placed at each end with the third in the centre, and the other two are wide-mouthed beakers.

Gu   The origin of the Transitional beaker vase shape may be found in the bronze *gu* ritual drinking goblets of the Shang dynasty.

Guan   A large heavy jar with widening body and short neck, sometimes with cover, originally used for storing food.

Gui   The *gui* shape without handles can be traced back to bronze ritual food containers of the 12th–11th century B.C.

Hard paste   Porcelain produced from the appropriate proportions of *gao ling* and *bai dunzi* and fired to a temperature of about 1,250°C. to produce vitrification and translucency.

Imperial yellow   A collector's term for yellow monochrome wares produced from the Chenghua period onward. The colour does, however, have a ritual significance, pieces of this colour being used on the altars dedicated to the Earth, Agriculture and Sericulture, etc. The yellow colour is derived from iron or antimony, the latter giving a purer and often brighter colour than iron, which usually has a slightly brownish tinge.

Iron-red   An enamel colour derived from an iron sulphate; it is also called 'coral-red'. The colour is used either as a self-colour or in combination with other enamel colours. Like all enamel colours, it is fired in a muffle kiln.

Jesuit China   This is a term for which there is no foundation in fact, but which originated in the belief that this ware, decorated with Western designs, was produced under the influence of the Jesuit missionaries. The earliest wares of this kind were produced in the Kangxi period and were blue and white, apparently executed at Jingdezhen; the later wares of the type, mostly plates and saucers, were copied from engravings of biblical or classical scenes, in black or sepia enamels with touches of gold; a few polychrome-enamelled examples are also known. Most of these last date from the Qianlong period, though a few may be earlier.

Jingdezhen   The great ceramic centre in the province of Jiangxi in southern China where the Imperial wares were produced regularly from the beginning of the Ming Dynasty, at the end of the fourteenth century. The kilns had certainly been in operation long before this time, but it is not known how early they started. The district is exceptionally rich in all the raw materials for the manufacture of porcelain, and production still continues today.

Kaolin   *(see Gao ling)*

Kendi   A drinking vessel with bulbous body, tall neck and mammiform spout designed for drinking without touching the vessel to the lips. The shape was also adapted for use as a *hookah* or water pipe base.

Key fret   A repeating design used as a band or a filler, found on ceramics, lacquer and cloisonné.

Kraak porcelain   The name given to a type of blue and white porcelain produced in the Wanli period and first half of the seventeenth century. The name may derive from the Dutch name for a Portuguese ship, a *carrack,* one of which was captured in 1603 while carrying a rich cargo that included this type of ware. Kraak porcelain was the first Chinese ware to reach Europe in any quantity, and it had a profound influence on the history of European ceramics. The designs were quickly copied by the potters of Delft and later at many other centres in Europe.

Lappets   Often called 'ruyi lappets', this motif resembles the head of the curved *ruyi* sceptre, a ceremonial object carried by certain Buddhist deities and an emblem of monastic authority. The motif itself is nearly heart-shaped and occurs commonly as a repeating band pattern. It is very similar, on a small scale, to the cloud-collar motif for which the term 'lappets' is often, and perhaps mistakenly, used.

Lead glaze   A glaze material containing silica in the form of sand or quartz, fused by means of an oxide of lead. It fires at a low temperature (about 800°C.) and may be used on pottery, but not on porcelain unless it has first been fired without glaze to the usual high temperature required for this material, approximately 1,200-1,250°C.

Lingzhi   The sacred fungus, identified as *Polyporus lucidus,* symbolic of longevity. It occurs in decoration with other longevity symbols such as the peach, the crane and the pine tree.

Lotus panels   A decoration used mainly as a border motive, either upright or pendant. It derives ultimately from the lotus petals of the Buddhist lotus throne *(padmasana).*

Manzus   The Manzu or Jurchen tribes were from the region north-west of Liaotung beyond the Great Wall and close to the Korean border, later to become known as Manchuria. They were not nomadic steppe-dwellers like the Mongols, but lived by a mixture of hunting, grazing and farming. They crossed the Great Wall and captured Beijing in 1644, establishing the Qing dynasty which was to rule China until 1911.

Martaban   Large, high-fired stoneware storage jar, often covered in olive green or brown lustrous glazes. The name 'martaban' has nothing to do with the entrepot port of that name on the coast of Burma. Believed to have been made in China over several centuries, they are extremely difficult to date with any precision but were probably made from the Yuan period until the early Qing dynasty, and were used as resilient containers to ship staple foods, oils and drinking water on the South Asian trading routes.

Meisande   A Japanese term for a type of Kraak dish on which the sides are decorated with petal-shaped cartouches (Pl. 47) rather than the usual radial panels (Pl. 45).

Oxidizing conditions   These conditions are achieved by allowing as much air as possible to enter the kiln during firing; under such conditions, glazes containing iron oxides become yellow, brown or black.

Peach bloom   A reduced copper glaze effect developed in the Kangxi period.

Petuntse   *(see Bai dunzi)*

Powder blue   Cobalt blue was blown on to the raw body of the clay through a bamboo tube closed at the end with fine gauze; the piece was then glazed. The technique was introduced in the Tianqi period, but only fully developed in the Kangxi period.

Qilin   The fabulous creature called the Chinese unicorn. It may be leonine, with scales and horns, or it may be an elegant cloven-footed beast, with or without scales, with a bushy mane and tail, and a horn or a pair of horns. Variations are extremely numerous and impossible to classify satisfactorily as the Chinese have in the past given this name to many animals, including the giraffe.

Reducing conditions   These are conditions produced by cutting down the air supply to the kiln during firing, to such an extent that carbon dioxide is reduced to carbon monoxide, compelling the fire to absorb oxygen for combustion purposes from the constituents of the glaze. This process accounts for the blues, greens, greys and lavender tones of Song period wares, and copper-reds of the fourteenth century onward.

Reign marks   These *nian hao* are inscriptions, generally in underglaze blue, but also in overglaze red or blue enamel, consisting of four or six characters giving the title of the regnal period during which the piece is purported to have been made. Marks do not normally occur before the fifteenth century and should always be regarded with reserve.

Ruyi   *(see Lappets)*

Seal mark   A reign mark, generally in underglaze blue but sometimes in red or blue enamel, written in an archaic manner similar to that used on a man's personal seal, which was usually rectangular or square.

Slip   A white firing clay diluted to a thick creamy consistency and used as a surface dressing, for white-painted or trailed decoration, and for joining parts or clay reliefs to the body of a vessel.

Supercargo   The business agent of a Western company trading overseas. The supercargo would travel as a passenger on the merchant ship chartered by the company for its trading voyage, and would be responsible for all its trading transactions.

Swatow wares   An attractive and robust group of wares from Fujian Province, boldly decorated in red, turquoise, black, blue and white enamels. Other types include slip-decorated wares with pale blue, brown or celadon-type glazes. The pieces are commonly large and roughly finished, with much sand and grit adhering to the glazed base. They were exported to Japan, South-East Asia, Indonesia and India in the late sixteenth and seventeenth centuries. The name comes from one of the ports through which the ware passed out of China.

Three Abundances   The peach, the pomegranate and persimmon, symbolic of long life, numerous progeny and happiness; the persimmon is sometimes replaced by the finger citron.

Three Friends   Prunus, pine and bamboo, all emblems of longevity and of winter, are also symbolic of the qualities of the gentleman. The prunus is associated with good looks and sturdy independence, in that it flowers at a time when nothing else appears to grow. The pine is symbolic of the constancy of friendship in times of adversity, and of endurance. Bamboo, known for durability, is symbolic of the integrity of the scholar and gentleman who remains loyal in adversity. These three also represent the three religions of China: Daoism, Buddhism and Confucianism.

Transitional   The Transitional period is taken as commencing from the death of the emperor Wanli in 1620, when Pan Xiang the eunuch commissioner responsible for supervising the Imperial orders at Jingdezhen was withdrawn, until Tang Yingxuan was appointed as superintendent by the emperor Kangxi in 1683. The loss of Imperial patronage during this period allowed more freedom for the potteries producing the best wares to manufacture for the export and domestic markets, and led to the introduction of new styles.

Trellis pattern   A repeating geometrical pattern used for borders, or as a filler. There are several forms of it.

Underglaze blue   Cobalt blue pigment applied directly to the body, before glazing and firing. This was the usual technique used in the production of Chinese blue and white wares. The pigment was extracted from two types of cobaltiferous ore: Mohammedan blue, an imported ore containing arsenic as a impurity; and native cobalt, containing manganese as an impurity instead of arsenic.

VOC   The abbreviated version of the Verenigde Oost-Indische Companie, the international monopolist trading company of the United Provinces (The Netherlands).

Water dropper   A small vessel with only a small hole, for gently shaking water on to an ink-stone or paint palette.

Willow pattern   This is, in fact, an English interpretation of a Chinese story set in a landscaped pleasure ground. It first appeared on blue transfer-printed earthenware.

Wucai   'Five colours' is a term applied to porcelains of the Ming and Qing dynasties decorated in overglaze enamel colours, often with coarsely handled underglaze blue combined with red, green, yellow, aubergine and black, and occasionally with a clear turquoise enamel as well. The outlines of the designs are drawn in overglaze black, dark brown or red enamel, so that the type is easily distinguished from Doucai.

Yixing   Potteries in Jiangsu Province, not far from Shanghai, still in production, are believed to have started operating in the sixteenth century. The kilns are best known in the West for their reddish-brown unglazed stonewares, the tea pots being especially famous. The decoration is usually either engraved, or in low relief.

Zhadou   A wide-mouthed jar used for depositing bones and scraps of food at the dinner table.

SELECTED BIBLIOGRAPHY

Ashmolean Museum, *Eastern Ceramics and Other Works of Art from the Collection of Gerald Reitlinger*, exhibition catalogue, Oxford, 1981.

Bayne-Powell, R., *Housekeeping in the 18th Century*, John Murray, London, 1956.

Butler, Sir Michael, 'Chinese Porcelain at the End of the Ming', *Transactions of the Oriental Ceramic Society*, London, 1983–4.

Butler, Sir Michael, 'Chinese Porcelain at the Beginning of the Qing', *Transactions of the Oriental Ceramic Society*, London, 1985–6.

Butler, Sir Michael, *Chinese Porcelain: The Transitional Period, 1620–1683*, exhibition catalogue, Princesshof Museum, Leeuwarden, 1986.

Christie's Amsterdam, sale catalogues: 7 December 1983, Lots 351–431; 14 March 1984, also Additional Lots 587-1 to 587-75; 12–13 June 1984, also Additional Lots 599-1 to 1323; 14 February 1985; *The Nanking Cargo: Chinese Export Porcelain and Gold*, 28 April–2 May 1986.

Clair, C., *Kitchen and Table*, Abelard and Schuman, New York, 1965.

Clayton, M., *The Collector's Dictionary of Gold and Silver*, Antique Collectors' Club, revised edition, 1985.

Crossman. C.L. *The China Trade*, Pyne Press, Princeton, 1972.

Curtis, Julia, 'Transition Ware Made Plain: A Wreck from the South China Sea', *Oriental Art*, Vol.XXXI, No. 2, Summer 1985.

Detweiler, S.G., *George Washington's Chinaware*, Abrams, New York, 1982.

Dillon, Michael, 'A History of the Porcelain Industry in Jingdezhen', PhD dissertation, University of Leeds, 1976.

Donnelly, P.J., *Blanc de Chine*, Faber, London, 1969.

Du Boulay, A., *Christie's Pictorial History of Chinese Ceramics*, Phaidon-Christie's, Oxford, 1984.

Feng-chun Ma, 'De Hatcher Collectie: Kraakporselein en Overgangsgoed/afkomstig uit een Scheepswrak', MA thesis, Department of Art History and Archaeology of East-Asia, University of Amsterdam, June 1985.

Ferris, Alice M., '17th Century Transitional Porcelains. The Development of Landscape Painting', *Oriental Art*, Vol. XIV, No.3, Autumn 1968.

Foster, W., *The East India House*, Bodley Head, London, 1924.

Godden, G.A., *Oriental Export Market Porcelain*, Granada, London, 1979.

Howard, D.S., and Ayers, J., *China for the West*, Sotheby Parke Bernet Publications, London, 1978.

Hsu Wen-chin, 'Fictional Scenes on Chinese Transitional Porcelain (1620–c.1683) and their Sources of Decoration', Museum of Far Eastern Antiquities, Bulletin No. 58, Stockholm, 1986.

Jenyns, R. Soame, 'The Wares of the Transitional Period between the Ming and the Qing, 1620–1683', Archives of the Chinese Art Society of America, Vol. IX, 1955.

Jenyns, R. Soame, *Later Chinese Porcelain*, Faber, London, 1965.

Jorg, C.J.A., *Porcelain and the Dutch China Trade*, Martinus Nijhoff, The Hague, 1982.

Jorg, C.J.A., *The Geldermalsen: History and Porcelain*, Kemper, Gröningen, 1986.

Jourdain, M., and Jenyns, R. Soame, *Chinese Export Art in the Eighteenth Century*, Country Life, London, 1950.

Kilburn, Richard, *Transitional Wares and their Forerunners*, exhibition catalogue, Oriental Ceramic Society of Hong Kong, 1981.

Krahl, Regina, *Chinese Ceramics in the Topkapi Saray Museum, Istanbul*, 3 vols, Sotheby Parke Bernet Publications, London, 1986.

Little, Stephen, *Chinese Ceramics of the Transitional Period: 1620–1683*, exhibition catalogue, China Institute in America, New York, 1983.

Little, Stephen, 'Chinese Porcelains of the Chongzhen Period: 1628–1644', *Oriental Art*, Vol. XXIX, No. 2, Summer 1983.

Lunsingh Scheurleer, D.F., *Chinese Export Porcelain*, English translation, Faber, London, 1974.

Marchant, S. and Son, *Chinese Blue and White – Wanli to K'ang Hsi*, exhibition catalogue, London, 1980.

Medley, M., *A Handbook of Chinese Art*, Bell & Hyman, London, 1977.

Miedema. H., *Kraak Porselein en Overgangsgoed*, Princessshof Museum, Leeuwarden, 1964.

Morse, H.B., *The Chronicles of the East India Company Trading to China, 1635-1834*, Clarendon Press, Oxford, 1926.

Palmer, A., *Movable Feasts*, Oxford University Press, London, 1953.

Raffald, E., *The Experienced English Housekeeper*, facsimile edition, E. and W. Books, London, 1970.

Rinaldi, Maura, 'Kraak Porcelain: The History and Classification of Dishes', *Heritage,* No.8, National Museum, Singapore, 1986.

Smith, E., *The Compleat Housewife*, facsimile edition, Library Services Publications Ltd, London, 1968.

Spriggs, Arthur I., 'Red Cliff Bowls of the Late Ming Period', *Oriental Art,* Vol. VII, No.4, Winter 1961.

Spriggs, Arthur I., 'Oriental Porcelains in Western Paintings, 1450–1700', *Transactions of the Oriental Ceramic Society,* Vol. 36, London, 1964–6.

Spriggs, Arthur I., 'Transitional Porcelain Ginger Jars', *Oriental Art*, Vol. XI, No.2, Summer 1965.

Toppin, Aubrey J., 'The China Trade and Some London Chinamen', *Transactions of the English Ceramic Circle*, London, 1934.

Van der Pijl-Ketel, C.L., *The Ceramic Load of the Witte Leeuw (1613)*, Rijksmuseum, Amsterdam, 1982.

Volker, T., *Porcelain and the Dutch East India Company, 1602-1682*, Rijksmuseum voor Volkenkunde, Leiden, 1971.

CHRONOLOGY

The Coming of the Europeans to South-East Asia

1498   First arrival of the Portuguese in South-East Asia

1511   Portuguese capture of Malacca

1514   First visit to China coast by Portuguese

1557   Founding of Macao

1570   Spanish capture of Manila

1580   Merging of Spanish and Portuguese crowns under Philip II of Spain (until 1640)

1596   First Dutch voyage to South-East Asia

1600   British East India Company (EIC) founded (the so-called 'London Company')

1601   First EIC voyage to South-East Asia

1602   Dutch East India Company (VOC) founded

1621   VOC South-East Asian regional headquarters established in Java at Batavia

1624   VOC transhipment trading station established at Fort Zeelandia, Taiwan

1644   Collapse of the Ming dynasty and official dynastic establishment of the Qing (Manzu) invaders

1645   Continuing Civil War in southern China; pro-Ming loyalists rebel in Fujian Province

1657   Coxinga rebellion and related piracy renders impossible Dutch trading from Fort Zeelandia

1662-1722   Emperor Kangxi inspires artistic and scientific revival, with initial Western Jesuit influence

1683   Jingdezhen kilns receive a new Imperially nominated Director

1708-9   Amalgamation of the 'London Company' and 'New Company' to form the 'Honourable English East India Company'

1746   Zeeland Chamber of the VOC commissions six new ships, including the *Geldermalsen*

August 1748   The *Geldermalsen* leaves for Batavia, Canton, Japan and India

18 Dec 1751   The *Geldermalsen* leaves Canton, bound for Holland via the Cape of Good Hope

3 Jan 1752   The *Geldermalsen* hits uncharted reef

1752   VOC merchantman *Bredenhof* leaves Zeeland bound for Bengal

1759   Co-Hong merchant guild in Canton revived to monopolize and superintend trade with Westerners

Dec 1783-1784   First American ships set out to trade directly with China at Canton

1791   English East India Company discontinues importation of Chinese porcelain

Chinese Dynasties and Reigns

Song	**960–1279**
Northern Song	960–1127
Southern Song	1127–1279
Liao	**916–1125**
Jin	**1115–1234**
Yuan	**1271–1368**
Ming	**1368–1644**
Hongwu	1368–1398
Jianwen	1399–1402
Yongle	1403–1424
Hongxi	1425
Xuande	1426–1435
Zhengtong	1436–1449
Jingtai	1450–1456
Tianshun	1457–1464
Chenghua	1465–1487
Hongzhi	1488–1505
Zhengde	1506–1521
Jiajing	1522–1566
Longqing	1567–1572
Wanli	1573–1620
Taichang	1620
Tianqi	1621–1627
Chongzhen	1628–1644
Qing	**1644–1911**
Shunzhi	1644–1661
Kangxi	1662–1722
Yongzheng	1723–1735
Qianlong	1736–1795

INDEX